Quick JavaScript

Are you an experienced programmer who wants to get started quickly in JavaScript and the HTML DOM? This is your book.

Do you need encyclopedic knowledge of JavaScript and/or the HTML DOM? This book is not for you.

Are you a novice who wants to learn to program? This book is not for you. In fact, this language is not for you. Get a good Python book.

This book will get you programming in JavaScript as quickly as possible. In addition, it will provide you with a basic understanding of the Document Object Model, the massive data structure used to represent web pages. With these tools, you will be able to build interactive web pages.

If you program in C++ or Java, there are parts of the book you can skip over because the JavaScript statements are exactly the same. These parts are clearly marked.

JavaScript is the language—the *only* language—used by browsers. To create interactive web pages, you need to know both JavaScript and the DOM. This book will get you started.

Quick JavaScript

David Matuszek

CRC Press
Taylor & Francis Group
Boca Raton London New York

CRC Press is an imprint of the
Taylor & Francis Group, an **informa** business

A CHAPMAN & HALL BOOK

First edition published 2023
by CRC Press
6000 Broken Sound Parkway NW, Suite 300, Boca Raton, FL 33487-2742

and by CRC Press
4 Park Square, Milton Park, Abingdon, Oxon, OX14 4RN

CRC Press is an imprint of Taylor & Francis Group, LLC

© 2023 David Matuszek

Library of Congress Cataloging-in-Publication Data
Names: Matuszek, David L., author.
Title: Quick JavaScript / David Matuszek.
Description: First edition. | Boca Raton: CRC Press, [2023]
| Series: Quick programing | Includes bibliographical references and index.
Identifiers: LCCN 2022046807 | ISBN 9781032417578 (hbk)
| ISBN 9781032417561 (pbk) | ISBN 9781003359609 (ebk)
Subjects: LCSH: JavaScript (Computer program language)
| Computer programming.
Classification: LCC QA76.73.J39 M385 2023
| DDC 005.2/762--dc23/eng/20221202
LC record available at https://lccn.loc.gov/2022046807

ISBN: 978-1-032-41757-8 (hbk)
ISBN: 978-1-032-41756-1 (pbk)
ISBN: 978-1-003-35960-9 (ebk)

DOI: 10.1201/9781003359609

Typeset in Minion
by SPi Technologies India Pvt Ltd (Straive)

*To all my students
past, present, and future*

Contents

Author

I'm David Matuszek, known to most of my students as "Dr. Dave."

I wrote my first program on punched cards in 1963 and immediately got hooked.

I taught my first computer classes in 1970 as a graduate student in computer science at the University of Texas at Austin. I eventually earned a PhD there, and I've been teaching ever since. Admittedly, I spent over a dozen years in industry, but even then I taught as an adjunct for Villanova University.

I finally escaped from industry and joined the Villanova faculty full time for a few years, and then moved to the University of Pennsylvania, where I directed a master's program (MCIT, Masters in Computer and Information Technology) for students coming into computer science from another discipline.

Throughout my career, my main interests have been in artificial intelligence (AI) and programming languages. I've used a *lot* of programming languages.

I retired in 2017, but I can't stop teaching, so I'm writing a series of "quick start" books on programming and programming languages. I've also written two science fiction novels, *Ice Jockey* and *All True Value*, and I expect to write more. Check them out!

If you found this book useful, it would be wonderful if you would post a review. Reviews, even critical ones, help to sell books.

And, hey, if you're a former student or colleague, drop me a note at david.matuszek@gmail.com. I'd love to hear from you!

Preface

If you are a programmer who wants to get started programming in JavaScript as quickly as possible, this book is for you.

If you are hoping to learn JavaScript as your first programming language, this book is **not** for you.

If you want a comprehensive encyclopedia of JavaScript, this book is **not** for you. For that, let me recommend the excellent *JavaScript: The Definitive Guide* (David Flanagan, O'Reilly).

Versions of JavaScript

JavaScript is an evolving language. It is defined by a series of standards known as *ECMAScript* by Ecma International.

As a language, JavaScript looks much like Java or C++. Unlike these languages, the original version of JavaScript is widely regarded as a hastily written, poorly designed language. Because of this perception, other languages have been written for use on HTML pages (CoffeeScript, Dart, etc.), but these must be compiled to JavaScript in order to be used by browsers. JavaScript is the only language understood by browsers.

In order to make significant changes to the JavaScript language without breaking existing programs, ECMAScript 2015 introduced *strict mode*. Strict mode eliminates or modifies the worst parts of JavaScript. All new programming should be done in strict mode.

To invoke strict mode for an entire program, put "use strict"; (complete with quotes) at the first line of a program. To invoke strict mode for a single function, put that string as the first line inside the function.

The primary use of JavaScript is to add interactivity to web pages. Web pages are written in *HTML, HyperText Markup Language*. This book is not about HTML, but it does cover the minimum necessary.

When running in a browser, JavaScript cannot do arbitrary file I/O, nor can it communicate with web servers other than the one from which it came. This is necessary for security; you do not want web pages to access your files without your knowledge. Other environments, such as IDEs, may allow these operations.

CHAPTER 1

Introduction

1.1 HELLO, WORLD!

Traditionally, the first program to be written in a new language is one that prints out "Hello, World!" We will follow that tradition.

The one line of JavaScript needed is:

```
alert("Hello, World!");
```

To execute this code, we have several options.

- Put it in a web page and run it in a browser.

- Run it in an *IDE* (*Integrated Development Environment*).

- Run it from an editor application.

- Run it from an online JavaScript editor.

1.2 JAVASCRIPT IN THE BROWSER

If you save the following text in a file and then open the file in a browser, an alert dialog containing the text "Hello, World!" will appear.

 DOI: 10.1201/9781003359609-1

```
<!DOCTYPE html>
<html>
  <head>
    <title>Using JavaScript</title>
  </head>
  <body>
    <script>
      alert("Hello, World!");
    </script>
  </body>
</html>
```

- The <!DOCTYPE html> tag says that this is an HTML document.

- The entire page is enclosed in the "container" <html> down to </html>. Tags beginning with "</" denote the end of a container. In this example, only the !DOCTYPE tag is not a container.

- The <title> tag contains the text that will be displayed in the header bar of the page.

- The HTML document is divided into two parts: The <head> contains assorted information that is not displayed and the <body> contains the part that is displayed.

- The <script> tag contains the JavaScript code. Typically, JavaScript functions are defined in <script> tags in the <head> and calls to them are made in <script> tags or in "event handlers" in the <body>.

1.3 BROWSER CONSOLES

To run JavaScript, you can use any text editor to include it in <script> tags in an HTML page, and load the page into any browser.

This is not the best way to write programs. Browsers are designed to *ignore* errors; after all, the user doesn't want to see them. You, on the other hand, want to see them and correct them. For this you need to open your browser's *console*. A console will display error messages (among other things).

To open the console:

- In most browsers: Press F12.

- In Safari (Macintosh): Go to Preferences: Advanced and check Show Develop menu in menu bar. Once this is done, use cmd-opt-C to show the console.

Browser consoles have a number of features to assist in programming and debugging. These vary and take some time to learn; they are not covered in this book.

1.4 RUNNING JAVASCRIPT

There are several IDEs (Integrated Development Environments) that can be used for JavaScript. **Visual Studio Code** is perhaps the most popular; it is cross-platform and free. (Don't confuse this with **Visual Studio**, which is neither cross-platform nor free.) **NetBeans** and **Eclipse** (with a suitable plugin) are other popular IDEs.

Some editors can be configured to run JavaScript on command. This can be a convenient way to run JavaScript programs that consist of a single file. **Sublime Text** (cross-platform) and **Notepad++** (Windows and Linux) are examples.

Yet another alternative is to use an online JavaScript editor. A search for "JavaScript online" will find several of these; jsfiddle.net is one I have used extensively. They differ in features, but most will display both output and console. Since they run in a browser, JavaScript code written there has limited ability to do file I/O.

Finally, all the major browsers have a "developer mode" so that code can be written and tested directly in the browser.

1.5 GETTING INPUT

There are two functions that will ask for input from the user:

- *result* = prompt(*prompt*, *default*);

    - This displays the *prompt* in a modal dialog box, with a place for the user to enter text. The second parameter is optional; if given, it will be shown in the text field.

    - The dialog box has two buttons: OK, to return the user's entry as a string, and Cancel, to return null.

- *result* = confirm(*question*);

    - This displays the *question* in a modal dialog box with two buttons: OK, to return true, and Cancel, to return false.

1.6 PRODUCING OUTPUT

There are several functions to display the results of your code. For browser use, remember to put your function calls inside <script>...</script> tags.

- alert(*arg*)

    - This is the simplest way to see a result. Calling alert with one argument of any type will pop up a dialog box containing the given value. There are two disadvantages: The dialog box is modal, which means that it must be dismissed before computation can continue; and you only get to see one message at a time.

- console.log(*args*)

    - If you have a console open, this method will display something on it, but exactly what it displays is highly implementation dependent. It may display the *args* separated by spaces or by newlines, or it may display only the first argument. Try it to see what it does in whatever console you prefer to use.

- Since console.log is intended primarily for debugging, most implementations will display the actual structure of the *args*, without using the toString method.

- The console has a number of other methods, such as clear() and trace(). Implementation varies.

• document.write(*args*)

- This will write its arguments to the body of the HTML. If executed as the page is being loaded, it writes the arguments directly in that location. But if write is called *after* the body has been loaded (for example, from a function), the call *replaces* the entire HTML body; this is probably not what you want.

• document.writeln(*args*)

- This acts just like write, except that the method writes a newline after the last argument. Since HTML ignores newlines, this is fairly useless. To get a newline that isn't ignored, write the string "<br>".

The advantage of the alert and write methods is that they do not require you to have a console open in order to view results.

CHAPTER 2

JavaScript

The Bare Minimum

This chapter and Chapter 3 describe JavaScript simply as a language, without reference to Web programming. It is in two major parts:

The Bare Minimum—This section is intended to get you started programming in JavaScript as quickly as possible. The best way to do that is to try things out as you go.

In More Detail—This goes over the same material again, filling in a lot of the gaps. To some extent, it can also be used as a reference.

2.1 COMMENTS

// introduces a comment that extends to the end of the line.

Multi-line comments start with /* and end with */.

Inside a comment, // and /* have no special meaning (so you cannot "nest" comments). Inside a quoted string or regular expression, // and /* do not start a comment.

DOI: 10.1201/9781003359609-2

2.2 DATA TYPES

2.2.1 Primitives

There are eight data types:

- A *number* may be written with or without a decimal point, but all numbers are stored as double precision floating point.

- A *bigint* is an integer with an arbitrarily large number of digits.

- The two *boolean* values are written as true and false.

- A *string* may be enclosed in either single quotes, double quotes, or backticks (`). There is no "character" type.

- A *symbol* is a value that is guaranteed to be unique; no other value is equal to it. A symbol is created by calling Symbol() or Symbol(*name*), where *name* is a (not necessarily unique) value that may be helpful in debugging.

- The *undefined* type has a single value, undefined. It is the value of a variable that has been declared but not yet given a value.

- The *null* type has a single value, null, meaning that the value does not exist.

- An *object* is any more complicated data type. Functions, arrays, sets, maps, regular expressions, errors, and dates are all special types of object, as are user-defined objects.

The type of a value can be determined by typeof, which can be used as either an operator, typeof *x*, or as a function, typeof(*x*). It will return, as a string, one of the type names given above (for example, "number").

There are two exceptions to the above.

- The value of typeof(null) is "object". This is generally regarded as an error in the design of the language.

- For any type of object except a function, typeof will return "object". Applied to a function, typeof will return "function".

2.2.2 User-Defined Objects

An *object* is a collection of named values, called its *properties*. You can define an object by putting *property*: *value* pairs inside braces and later refer to the values with the syntax *object*. *property*. For example,

```
let friend = { givenName: "Anna",
               surname: "Lang" };
alert("Hello, " + friend.givenName);
```

If the name of a property is stored in a variable or can be computed, it can be accessed by the syntax *object*[*expression*], for example, friend["given" + "Name"].

The test *property* in *object*, where *property* is given as a string, will return true if and only if *object* has that *property*. A request for a property that does not exist will get the value undefined.

2.2.3 Built-In Object Types

JavaScript comes with a number of built-in, or predefined, object types. Among these are arrays, sets, maps, dates, and regular expressions.

2.2.4 Arrays

An *array* is an ordered collection of values. An *array literal* can be defined by enclosing comma-separated values in square brackets:

```
let ary = ["cat", "dog", "mouse"];
```

Commas can be used either *between* values or *after* values, so the above assignment is exactly equivalent to:

```
let ary = ["cat", "dog", "mouse", ];
```

The last comma is sometimes called a ***trailing comma***.

Array indexing is zero-based; the first element of the above array is ary[0] and the last is ary[ary.length - 1].

Arrays of higher dimension can be created simply by nesting array literals:

```
let ary2d = [[11, 12], [21, 22]];
```

After the above assignment, ary2d[1] is [21, 22] and ary2d[1][0] is 21.

A less-often used form is Array(***values***):

```
let ary = new Array("cat", "dog", "mouse");
```

This form is not generally recommended. One odd feature of it is that if the argument is a single numeric value, Array(***n***), the result is a ***sparse array*** of ***n*** locations, *not* an array containing the single value ***n***.

In a sparse array, no storage is allocated for the elements of the array until they have been assigned values; unassigned locations will appear to have the value undefined. A sparse array can be arbitrarily large (only the actual values in it contribute to its size), but it is slower to work with.

The length property of an array is always one more than the largest index. Since an array may be sparse, length is not necessarily a count of the number of values in the array.

Arrays can be created from ***iterable types*** (types that can be stepped through).

- Array.from(***set***) — Returns an array containing the elements of ***set***.

- `Array.from(`*string*`)` — Returns an array of characters from *string*, each as a string.
- `Array.from(`*map*`)` — Returns an array of [*key, value*] arrays.
- `Array.from(`*array*`)` — Returns a (shallow) copy of *array*.

Arrays may contain a mix of different types of values.

2.2.5 Sets

A *set* is a collection of values, such that (1) no value appears more than once, and (2) the order in which the values occur in the set is irrelevant.

Operations are:

- `new Set(`*iter*`)` — Creates and returns a new set containing the values in the iterable object *iter* (often an array). To create an empty set, omit *iter*.
  - If *iter* is a map, the result is a set of [*key, value*] arrays.
- *set*`.has(`*value*`)` — Tests if *value* is a member of *set*.
- *set*`.add(`*value*`)` — Adds *value* to *set* if it is not already present, and returns *set*.
- *set*`.delete(`*value*`)` — If *value* is in *set*, it is deleted. `delete` does *not* return *set*; it returns `true` if *value* was in *set*, and `false` otherwise.
- *set*`.clear()` — Removes all values from *set* and returns `undefined`.
- *set*`.size` — Returns the number of elements in *set*.

2.2.6 Maps

Maps are lookup tables. Each entry in a map consists of a key-value pair. Keys must be unique, but the same value may occur multiple times.

Operations are:

- `new Map()` — Creates and returns a new, empty map.

- `new Map(`*array_or_set*`)` — The *array_or_set* must consist of [*key, value*] arrays; this returns a map with those keys and values.

- *map*`.has(`*key*`)` — Tests if *map* contains the given *key*.

- *map*`.set(`*key, value*`)` — Sets or changes the value associated with *key* to *value* and returns the modified *map*.

- *map*`.get(`*key*`)` — Returns the value associated with *key*, or undefined if *key* is not in the map.

- *map*`.delete(`*key*`)` — Removes *key* and its associated *value* from *map*. Returns true if *map* was changed, false if *key* wasn't found in *map*.

- *map*`.clear()` — Removes all values from *map* and returns undefined.

- *map*`.size` — Returns the number of key-value pairs in *map*.

Maps can use values of any type as keys.

Caution: The notations *map*`.`*value* and *map*`[`*value*`]` refer to map properties, not to map entries. Use set and get to access the entries.

2.2.7 Dates

JavaScript has a Date object, which can be created in any of the following ways:

- `new Date()` — Returns the current date and time in the browser's time zone.

- `new Date(`*ms*`)` — Returns the date that corresponds to the number of milliseconds since "epoch" (January 1, 1970).

- new Date(*year*, *month*, *day*, hours, *minutes*, *seconds*, *milliseconds*)

  - Up to five arguments may be omitted from the right end, for example, new Date(*year*, *month*, *day*).

  - You cannot supply just a year, because a single argument will be taken as milliseconds.

  - If the *year* is less than 100, 1900 will be added to it.

- new Date(*string*) — Converts *string* into a Date, if possible, and returns it. The International Standard format is *yyyy-mm-dd*, but many other formats are recognized.

Caution: Without new in front of it, Date() returns a string, not a date, and is equivalent to String(new Date()).

To access specific components of a Date object, use the following methods:

- *date*.getFullYear() and *date*.setFullYear(*year*)

  - *date*.setFullYear may also be given *month* and *day* arguments.

- *date*.getMonth() and *date*.setMonth(*n*), where *n* is 0 (January) to 11 (December).

- *date*.getDate() and *date*.setDate(*n*), where *n* is 1 to 31.

- *date*.getHours() and *date*.setHours(*n*), where *n* is 0 to 23.

- *date*.getMinutes() and *date*.setMinutes(*n*), where *n* is 0 to 59.

- *date*.getSeconds() and *date*.setSeconds(*n*), where *n* is 0 to 59.

- *date*.getMilliseconds() and *date*.setMilliseconds(*n*), where *n* is 0 to 999.

- *date*.getTime() and *date*.setTime(*n*), where *n* is milliseconds since epoch.

  - Date.now() also returns milliseconds since epoch but is shorter than new Date().getTime().

- *date*.getDay() returns 0 to 6, where 0 means Sunday (regardless of where you are, and despite ISO 8601 specifying Monday as the first day of the week).

Internally, Dates are kept as milliseconds since epoch. This makes arithmetic on dates very easy because the arguments to the various set methods are not limited to the same ranges as the get methods return. For example,

```
let date = new Date();
let day_of_month = date.getDate();
date.setDate(day_of_month + 100);
```

sets date to be a Date exactly 100 days in the future, with the correct month and year.

2.2.8 Regular Expressions

A *regular expression*, or *regexp*, defines a pattern to be applied to a string, to determine whether the pattern matches the string, or to search the string for substrings that do match.

Regular expressions are largely standardized, so all but the most idiosyncratic patterns can be used in JavaScript. In this section, we assume a knowledge of regular expressions and only describe how to use them in JavaScript. For the reader unfamiliar with regular expressions, there is a brief discussion in Appendix D.

A regular expression is written inside forward slashes, and may be followed by flags. For example, /[a-z]+/gi is the regular expression [a-z]+ with the global (g) and case-insensitive (i) flags. ([a-z]+ will match any sequence of lowercase letters.)

Parentheses are used to group parts of the regular expression. Groups are numbered left to right, starting with 1; an easy way to find the number of a group is to count only the left (opening) parentheses. Group 0 is the entire matched part. For example, in the pattern

```
a = "Call 1-800-555-1212 today!"
b = /1-800-((\d\d\d)-(\d\d\d\d))/
//  0       12      3
c = a.match(b)
```

The results will be

```
c[0] = "1-800-555-1212"
c[1] = "555-1212"
c[2] = "555"
c[3] = "1212"
```

The following methods can be used to apply regular expressions:

- **string**.search(**regexp**) — Returns the index of the start of the first substring in **string** that matches **regexp**, or null if no match is found. If the global modifier g is present, it is ignored.

- **string**.replace(**regexp**, **replacement**) — Searches **string** for **regexp** and, if found, replaces it with **replacement**. If the global modifier g is present, the method replaces all occurrences of **regexp** with **replacement**.

  - If **regexp** contains parenthesized groups, then **replacement** may use $1 to represent the first group matched, $2 to represent the second group matched, and so on.

- *string*.match(*regexp*) — Searches *string* for *regexp* and returns an array.

  - If the g flag is set, match returns an array of matched substrings, or null if no matches are found.

  - If the g flag is not set, match returns an array whose first element is the (first) matched substring and whose remaining elements, if any, are the substrings matched by each parenthesized group in *regex*. See the example at the beginning of this section.

- *string*.matchAll(*pattern*) – With the g flag, matchAll returns an iterator for each of the substrings of *string* that match *pattern*. This makes it convenient for use with a for/of loop.

- *string*. split(*regexp*) – Returns an array of substrings of *string*, where each occurrence of *regexp* separates the substrings in *string*.

The following are methods of *regexp* rather than of *string*.

- *regexp*.exec(*string*) – Searches *string* for *regexp* and remembers its position in *string*.

  - This method is designed to be used in a loop. If the g flag is set, each call of exec will return the next matching substring, or null when no more remain. After a null is returned, the *regex* is reset and can be used again.

  - If the g flag is not set, exec behaves like match without the g flag set.

- *regexp*.test(*string*) – Returns true if *regexp* matches somewhere in *string*, and null otherwise. The g flag is handled the same way that it is for exec.

2.3 IDENTIFIERS

Identifiers consist of letters, digits, underscores, and/or dollar signs; the first character may not be a digit.

By convention, variable and function names begin with a lowercase letter, while class names begin with a capital. The usual convention is to use "camel case" for multiword names, such as newUser. Constants are often written in all capital letters.

Keywords (if, true, class, etc.) cannot be used as identifiers.

2.4 LET AND CONST

JavaScript variables are *untyped*: Any variable can hold any type of value.

Variables are declared with the keyword let, along with an optional initial value; for example, let x or let x = 5. More than one variable can be declared in a let statement, for example,

```
let x = 5, y, z = 3; // leaves y undefined
```

Constants are declared with the word const and must be given a value at the time of declaration. Often the names of constants are written with all capital letters. For example,

```
const zero = 0;
const RED = "#FF0000";
```

Using a const *name* = *object*; declaration prevents any later assignment to *name*, so *name* will always refer to the same object, but it does not prevent changes to that object.

```
const card = {suit: "clubs", pips: 2};
card = {suit: "clubs", pips: 10}; // illegal
card.pips = 10; // legal
```

Variables declared with let or const at the top level of the program, not within any block, are global to the program; they can be accessed anywhere.

Variables and constants declared within a block have **block scope**. A **block** is a group of statements and/or expressions enclosed in braces, {...}. The **scope** of an identifier is that portion of the program in which the variable is visible and can be used.

In other words, variables and constants declared in a block are visible and can be used only in the innermost block in which they are declared. Outside that block, these variables and constants do not exist; their names can be recycled for other uses.

It is an error to attempt to get the value of a variable that has been declared but not yet given a value.

2.5 VAR

The modern way to declare a variable is with let. The older way, using var in place of let, or simply assigning a value to a variable, should be avoided. Variables declared the old way follow unusual, and generally undesirable, scope rules.

- It is not an error to use var to declare the same variable more than once in the same scope.

- The parameters to a function, and any variables declared with var inside that function, are local to the function. They may be used anywhere inside that function, even before the declaration. This is different from block scope.

- If a value is assigned to a new variable without declaring the variable with let, var or const, that variable has **global scope**: It can be used anywhere in the program.

  - This can only be done in **non-strict mode** (sometimes called "**sloppy mode**").

- If a variable has been declared with var but not assigned a value, it has the special value undefined.

2.6 OPERATORS

Here are the most common operators on numbers:

+ add

- subtract or unary minus

* multiply

/ divide, giving a floating-point result

% remainder (modulus)

** exponentiation

Common operators on booleans:

&& and

|| or

! not

Comparison operators, giving a boolean result:

< less than

<= less than or equal to

== equal to

=== strictly equal to (equal and same type)

!= not equal to

!== strictly unequal (different types or values)

>= greater than or equal to

> greater than

Caution: When comparing values of different types, JavaScript attempts to convert them to numbers. Despite the fact that undefined is converted to NaN and null is converted to 0, nevertheless undefined==null is true. Don't compare values if one or both of them could be null or undefined; check first using ===, which is always safe.

Caution: As in almost all languages, it is unwise to compare two floating point numbers for equality. For example, 11*(100/11) is not equal to 100, as these differ in the 14th decimal place. One potential workaround is to use the method .toFixed(*n*), which will return a *string* with *n* digits after the decimal point, then do string comparisons.

String *concatenation*:

+ concatenate (join together) two strings, or a string and any other value.

The arithmetic comparison operators can also be used on strings, giving lexicographic ordering. All capital letters precede all lowercase letters, thus "Cat" < "cat".

Assignment:

= *assignment operator*—can be used as an expression; the value of the expression is the value that is assigned.

JavaScript also has the + and - unary operators. The + operator, when applied to a non-numeric value (such as a string), attempts to convert that value into a number, returning NaN ("not a number") if it cannot.

?: The *ternary operator*: In the expression *test* ? *valueIfTrue*: *valueIfFalse*, the *test* determines which of the two succeeding values is used.

If you are familiar with Java, most of the Java operators can also be used in JavaScript, including all of the bit-manipulation operators. The bit-manipulation operators convert their operands to integers, do the operation on integers, and convert the results back to (floating-point) numbers.

Order of precedence is the same as in most languages: Unary plus and minus are done first, then exponentiation, then multiplication and division, then addition and subtraction, then assignment.

2.7 EQUALITY AND IDENTITY

The == and != comparison operators try to convert their operands to the same type. The results may be surprising. For example, 123, "123", [123], and even ["123"] are all considered equal when using ==.

The "strict" tests === and !== will regard values as unequal if they are of different types. Unless you want the automatic conversion, these operators should be preferred.

For objects (arrays, sets, etc.), the "equality" operators are actually tests of *identity*. That is, an object is "equal" only to itself, not to any other object. The comparison [1] == [1] is **false** because two arrays are created, then compared.

Assignment of objects does *not* create new objects. After the sequence a = [1]; b = a;, the test a == b will return true. This is because a and b are now references to the same object. Changes made to the object from either a or b will be visible to the other variable.

JavaScript has no built-in equality testing for objects; to do this, the objects need to be broken down into primitive components. This requires significant amounts of code. The sites underscorejs.com and lodash.com both provide large, well-tested libraries for this and other purposes.

2.8 CONVERSIONS

JavaScript performs most *conversions* (also called *coercions*) automatically. Here are some that might require some care.

Any arithmetic performed on primitives will cause them to be converted to numbers. Strings of digits will be converted in the obvious way. Boolean true will be converted to 1, null and false to 0, and undefined to NaN.

> **Exception**: The *binary* + operator is both addition and string concatenation, but concatenation has priority; 2 + "2" is "22". The *unary* operator + will attempt to convert its operand to a number, so 2 + +"2" is 4.

Any value in a boolean context (such as the condition of an if statement) will be treated as false if it is 0, undefined, null, NaN, or the empty string. All other values, including "0", are considered to be true.

When an array is converted to a string, the result is a string of comma-separated values; the brackets are omitted. Thus, a multidimensional array can readily be mistaken for a one-dimensional array.

2.9 STATEMENTS

Many statements in JavaScript are almost identical to those in Java. For the convenience of Java programmers, these statements are described separately from statements unique to JavaScript.

2.9.1 Semicolons

Every JavaScript statement should end with a semicolon. If you are used to programming in Java or one of the C languages, continue using semicolons the way you are used to.

Although each statement *should* be terminated by a semicolon, JavaScript uses a tool called *ASI* (*Automatic Semicolon Insertion*), which will, up to a point, put semicolons at the ends of lines where appropriate. If you miss a few semicolons it's probably okay, but it's unwise to depend on ASI to do this for you.

When a group of statements is enclosed in braces, {}, this forms a *compound statement* (or *block*). A semicolon is not needed after the closing brace.

If a statement needs to extend over two lines, separate it in a place where the first line cannot be understood as a complete statement. Good places to break a statement are after an operator or inside a parenthesized expression.

If a line begins with an opening parenthesis, opening bracket, or arithmetic operator, it will be taken as a continuation of the previous line. If this is not your intent, end the previous line with a semicolon.

Semicolons are required to separate two or more statements on the same line.

2.9.2 Declarations

Variables in JavaScript may hold any type of value, so their type is not a part of their declaration.

- `let x;`
- `var y = 5; // old style - avoid`
- `let z = 26;`
- `let a = 5, b = 10, c;`

It is an error to declare a variable more than once (except with var).

2.9.3 Function Definitions

A *function* is a block of code that can be *invoked* (called). The most common way of declaring a function is with this syntax:

```
function name (args) {
  statements
}
```

Functions in HTML should normally be defined in the <head> element to ensure that they will be defined before they are needed. Functions may be recursive. Functions may be nested within other functions.

Example definition:

```
function average(x, y) {
  let sum = x + y; // x, y, and sum are local
  return sum / 2;
}
```

Example call:

```
let avg = average(5, 10); // 7.5
```

Any variables declared within the function body are local to the function. The parameters are also local to the function.

Functions may access variables in the environment in which the function occurs (unless there is a local variable with the same name). All functions may access global variables. Functions declared within another function may access the variables available at the point of declaration.

Function definitions are *hoisted*. This simply means that all function definitions are processed before any other code is executed so that they need not lexically occur before calls to them can be made.

2.9.4 Familiar Statements

Many of the statements in JavaScript are identical to those in Java and C++. If you are experienced in one of those languages, feel free to skip ahead to Section 2.9.5, *JavaScript-Specific Statements*.

Note 1: While the traditional `for` statement is the same, its *initialization* part will, of course, use `let` rather than the type of the control variable.

Note 2: The `switch` statement allows each `case` to specify an expression, not just a constant value.

Here is a list of statements that are the same:

- *variable* = *expression*;

- *expression*;

- { *statements* }

- if (*condition*) {
    statements
  }

- if (*condition*) {
    statements
  } else {
    statements
  }

- while (*condition*) {
    statements
  }

- for (*initialization*; *condition*; *update*) {
    statements
  }

- do {
    statements
  } while (*condition*)

```
• switch (expression) {
    case expression:
      statements;
      break;
    case expression:
      statements;
      break;
    …
    default:
      statements;
  }
```

- *label*: *statement*;

- break;

- break *label*;

- continue;

- continue *label*;

- return *value*;

- return;

- ; // empty statement

2.9.4.1 Assignment Statements

An **assignment statement** gives a value to a variable. For example,

```
x = 5;
```

gives x the value 5.

The value of a variable may be changed. For example, the assignment statement

```
x = "abc";
```

will give x the new value "abc".

For each arithmetic operator *op*, the expression

```
variable op= expression;
```

is shorthand for

```
variable = variable op expression;
```

For example, x += 1; adds 1 to x.

2.9.4.2 Expressions

Any expression can be used as a statement; the value of the expression, if any, is discarded.

Expressions are allowed to act as statements because they can have side effects. For example, if a is an array, a.sort() sorts the array.

Expressions that return a result but do not have side effects can be used as statements, but they don't do anything. For example, using 2+2 as a statement is legal but useless.

This can lead to errors. If str is the string "Hello", the expression str.toUpperCase() returns the string "HELLO", and this can be assigned to a variable, but using str.toUpperCase() as a statement does nothing.

2.9.4.3 Compound Statements

A **compound statement**, or **block**, is some number (possibly zero) of declarations and statements, enclosed in braces, {}. A compound statement is itself considered to be a statement.

Control statements, such as if statements and loops, control the execution of a single statement. If you want to control more than just one statement, you must enclose those statements in braces to make them into a (single) compound statement.

The body of a function or method must always be a compound statement. (Exception: "arrow" functions, to be discussed later.)

Good style dictates that statements within a block be indented relative to the start of the block. The usual indentation for JavaScript is two spaces.

2.9.4.4 If Statements

An *if statement* tests a condition. If the condition is true, the following statement (typically, a compound statement) is executed. If the condition is not true, the if statement does nothing. The syntax is:

```
if (condition) {
  statements
}
```

For example, the following if statement resets x to zero if it has become negative.

```
if (x < 0) {
  x = 0;
}
```

An if statement may also have an else clause. If the condition is true, the statement following the condition is executed. If the condition is not true, the statement following the word else is executed. Both statements are typically compound statements. The syntax is:

```
if (condition) {
  some statements
}
else {
  some other statements
}
```

For example,

```
if (x % 2 == 0) {
  x = x / 2;
}
else {
  x = 3 * x + 1;
}
```

If either part contains only a single (non-compound) statement, the braces may be omitted. In this case, it is good style to put the single statement on the same line as the if or the else.

```
if (x % 2 == 0) x = x / 2;
else x = 3 * x + 1;
```

2.9.4.5 While Loops

A **while loop** is a loop with the test at the top. The syntax is:

```
while (condition) {
   statements
}
```

First, the **condition** is tested; if it is false, nothing more is done, and the loop exits without ever executing the **statements**. If the **condition** is true, the **statements** are executed, then the entire loop (starting with the test) is executed again.

For example, the approximate common log (that is, log base ten) of a number x can be computed by:

```
let log = 0;
while (x > 1) {
   x = x / 10;
   log = log + 1;
}
```

The braces indicate a block of statements. If there is only one statement, the braces may be omitted; however, it is good style to always include the braces.

Normally, the statements controlled by the loop must affect the condition being tested. In the above example, x is compared to 1, and the controlled statements change the value of x. If the controlled statements never make the condition false, then the loop never exits, and the program "hangs" (stops responding). This is a kind of error commonly, if inaccurately, called an **infinite loop**.

Two additional statement types, break and continue, can also control the behavior of while loops. These statements can be used with statement labels.

2.9.4.6 Do-While Loops

A ***do-while loop*** is a loop with the test at the bottom, rather than the more usual test at the top. The syntax is:

```
do {
   statements
} while (condition);
```

First, the ***statements*** are executed, then the ***condition*** is tested; if it is true, then the entire loop is executed again. The loop exits when the ***condition*** gives a false result.

This kind of loop is most often used when the test doesn't make any sense until the loop body has been executed at least once. For most purposes, the while loop is preferable.

For example, suppose you want to choose a random number between 0 and 1000 that is divisible by 7. You cannot test the number until after you have chosen it, so do-while is appropriate.

```
let x;
do {
   x = Math.round(1000 * Math.random());
} while (x % 7 != 0);
```

As with a while loop, an infinite loop will result if the exit condition is never satisfied.

The do-while loop is a little harder to think about than a while loop. Since we want a number that *is* divisible by 7, the loop has to test that the number *is not* divisible by 7.

Unlike other kinds of control statements, the braces in a do-while are required, even if only a single statement is in the loop.

The following code does *not* work:

```
do {
   let x = Math.round(1000 * Math.random());
} while (x % 7 != 0); // error
```

Variables declared within a block are local to that block. If the variable x is declared within the braces of the do-while loop, it cannot be used in the condition, which lies outside of the block.

Two additional statement types, break and continue, can also control the behavior of do-while loops. These statements can be used with statement labels.

2.9.4.7 Traditional For Loops

A *for loop* is a loop with the test at the top. The syntax is:

```
for (initialization; condition; update) {
   statements
}
```

The *initialization* is performed first, and only once. After that, the *condition* is tested and, if true, the *statements* are executed and the *update* is performed; then control returns to the *condition*. In other words, the for loop behaves almost exactly like the following while loop:

```
initialization;
while (condition) {
   statements;
   update;
}
```

The *initialization* may have one of the following forms:

- Assignment to a variable, for example, i = 0 or let i = 0.

- Assignment to more than one variable, separated by commas, for example let i = 0, j = 0; (this form is rarely used).

The word let, if used, must precede the first variable in the initialization.

The *update* is one of:

- An expression, typically an assignment statement such as i += 1. (An assignment statement is a kind of expression.)

- A comma-separated list of expressions, such as i += 1, j += 2.

The braces indicate a block of *statements*. If there is only one statement, the braces may be omitted; however, it is good style to always include the braces.

As an example, an array can be declared and its contents written out by:

```
let ary = [3, 1, 4, 1, 6];
for (let i = 0; i < ary.length; i += 1) {
    console.log(ary[i]);
}
```

Two additional statement types, break and continue, can also control the behavior of for loops. These statements, which will be described shortly, can be used with statement labels.

2.9.4.8 Scope in Loops
Consider:

for (let *variable* = *value*; *condition*; *update*) { *statements* }

The scope of *variable* is the entire for statement; it is not accessible outside this statement. If the keyword let is omitted, *variable* must have been declared previously; if let is replaced with var, *variable* is global.

When the loop body is a single statement, the braces are recommended but not required. In this case, it is good style to write the entire loop on a single line.

```
for (let variable = value; condition; update) statement;
```

The "block scope" of *variable* is the entire for statement, just as if the braces were present.

2.9.4.9 Switch Statements

Just as the if statement provides a choice between two blocks of code, based on a boolean value, the *switch statement* provides a choice between several blocks of code, based on a value of any type.

The syntax is fairly complex:

```
switch (expression) {
  case expression:
    statements;
    break;
  case expression:
    statements;
    break;
  ...
  case expression:
    statements;
    break;
  default:
    statements;
    break;
}
```

Operation is as follows. The switch *expression* is evaluated, and then compared against each case *expression* in order. When a case *expression* is found that is strictly equal to the switch *expression*, execution begins with the following statements and continues until either a break or a return is encountered, or until the end of the entire switch statement.

> **Note:** The === operator is used for the equality test. This will return a true result only if the two values are the same type as well as the same value.

The break statement is not required at the end of each case; if it is omitted, control will flow into the next group of statements. This is seldom what you want to happen. On the rare occasion that this is the desired behavior, it is best to include a comment that the omission is intentional, otherwise you or someone else may "correct" this apparent problem at some later date.

One case *expression*: may be followed immediately by another case *expression*: with no intervening statements (or break). If either *expression* matches the switch *expression*, the following *statements* will be executed.

The default case is optional and usually should come last. If no matching *expression* is found, the *statements* in the default case are executed. If no matching *expression* is found and there is no default case, the switch statement exits without doing anything.

It is good style to always include a default case, even if you believe that all possibilities have been covered.

The *statements* may be any sequence of zero or more statements. It is not necessary to use braces to group the statements (including the following break statement) into a compound statement, although this is sometimes done.

Here is a contrived example:

```
let v = 123.0;
let kind;
```

```
switch (v) {
  case 120 + 3:
    kind = "number";
    break;
  case "123":
    kind = "string";
    break;
  default:
    kind = "other";
}
console.log(v, "is a", kind);
```

This will result in the output 123 is a number, since the strict equality test makes no distinction between integers and floating point numbers; they are both of type number.

2.9.4.10 Labeled Statements
The syntax of a **labeled statement** is

identifier: **statement**;

Any statement may be labeled with an identifier, but it really only makes sense to label loop statements and switch statements. Labels are used in conjunction with the break and continue statements.

2.9.4.11 Break Statements
A **break statement** consists of the keyword break optionally followed by a statement label.

A break statement can only be used within a loop or a switch statement.

Execution of the break causes the enclosing loop or switch statement to exit. If the break statement is within nested loops and/or switch statements and does not have a label, only the immediately enclosing loop or switch statement is exited.

Execution of a break statement with a label causes the enclosing loop or switch statement with that label to exit, regardless of nesting level.

Given an array of numbers, consider the problem of finding two numbers such that one is exactly ten times the other. The following code solves this problem.

```javascript
let ary = [7, 30, 9, 20, 3, 5];
let i, j;
id: for (i = 0; i < ary.length; i += 1) {
    for (j = 0; j < ary.length; j += 1) {
        if (ary[i] == 10 * ary[j] && ary[i] != 0) {
            break id;
        }
    }
}
console.log(ary[i] + ", " + ary[j]);
```

Some programmers dislike the break statement, and indeed, there is usually a better way to solve a problem without using it.

2.9.4.12 Continue Statements

A **continue statement** consists of the keyword continue optionally followed by a statement label.

A continue statement can only be used within a loop. This is unlike a break statement, which can also be used within a switch statement.

Execution of the continue causes the enclosing loop to return to the test, or in the case of a traditional for loop, to the increment and then the test. Depending on the result, the loop may then continue or exit.

If the continue statement is within nested loops and does not have a label, control returns to the innermost loop. If it does have a label, control returns to the indicated loop.

The following code computes the sum of the values in the array, excluding strings.

```
let ary = [3, true, 4, false, 10, "hello"];
let sum = 0;
for (let i = 0; i < ary.length; i += 1) {
  if (typeof(ary[i]) == "string") continue;
  sum = sum + ary[i];
}
```

This code sets sum to 18, not 17, because true is counted as 1 and false is counted as 0.

While there is nothing actually wrong with the continue statement, refactoring the code to remove it almost always results in a simpler and more understandable program.

2.9.4.13 Return Statements

When a function is called, it typically executes some code and then returns some value to the calling location.

A function can return in one of four ways:

- It can reach the end of the function body and return the special value undefined;

- It can execute a return statement that has no following expression and return the special value undefined;

- It can execute a return statement with an expression, evaluate that expression, and return the result as the value of the function; or

- It can throw an exception, in which case the value is irrelevant.

The syntax of the return statement is either simply

```
return;
```

or

```
return expression;
```

Functions that are called for their side effects rather than for their value are sometimes called **procedures**.

2.9.4.14 Empty Statements

Although of very limited use, JavaScript does allow the use of an **empty statement** consisting of a semicolon by itself. The following statements are equivalent:

```
for (n = 1; n < 1000; n = 2 * n) {}
```

and

```
for (n = 1; n < 1000; n = 2 * n);
```

Either statement results in n being set to 1024.

2.9.5 JavaScript-Specific Statements

2.9.5.1 For/of

The **for/of loop** can be used for **arrays**, **sets**, **maps**, and **strings**. It has the syntax

```
for (let element of object) {
  statement;
}
```

- For arrays, the **element**s are the values in the array.

- For sets, the **element**s are the elements of the set.

- For maps, each **element** is an array of [**key**, **value**] arrays.

- For strings, the **element**s are the individual characters in the string.

The for/of loop can only be used to loop over iterable objects. User-defined objects are not iterable unless code is added to make them iterable.

2.9.5.2 For/in

The *for/in loop* can be used for user-defined **objects**, **arrays**, and **strings**. It has the syntax:

```
for (let element in object) {
  statement;
}
```

- For objects, the *element*s are the (enumerable) property names; the value of a property can be accessed with *object*[*element*].

- For arrays, the *element*s are the indices, along with any properties that may have been assigned to the array; the value can be accessed with *object*[*element*].

  - The for/in loop treats arrays like any other object. It is much slower than a for/of loop.

- For strings, the *element*s are the indices; the individual characters can be accessed with *object*[*element*].

An object may have non-enumerable, "hidden" properties, and a sparse array may have "missing" elements. These are skipped over by the for/in loop.

2.9.5.3 Throw

The programmer can use the ***throw statement*** to deliberately cause an exception. There is no "Exception" type—any type of value may be "thrown."

Note: JavaScript makes no distinction between "errors" and "exceptions."

The throw statement "throws" the exception to somewhere else, so as not to clutter up the normal execution of the program with code to handle (hopefully rare) exceptional conditions. The purpose of the try/catch statement (described in Section 2.9.5.4) is to catch a thrown exception.

The throw statement has the syntax:

throw *expression*;

where *expression* can be any type, but is typically an error number, an error message, or (as is the case with predefined exceptions), an object with name and message properties.

What happens to the thrown exception?

- If an exception occurs in the try portion of a try-catch-finally statement, the catch part handles the exception.

- Otherwise, if an exception occurs in a function, the function will return immediately to the point at which the function was called. Execution continues as if the exception was thrown at that point (which may involve returning up another level in a nest of function calls).

- Otherwise, if an exception occurs in top-level code, or hasn't been handled by the time the exception reaches the top level, it is up to the system to do something about it. In an IDE, the exception will be reported to the programmer. In a browser, the exception will probably be ignored.

2.9.5.4 Try-catch-finally

The ***try-catch-finally statement*** is used to separate error handling code from code that handles the "normal" case. This statement works exactly like the corresponding statement in Java, but with two minor syntactic differences.

- The try-catch-finally statement can have only one catch clause.

- The (*variable*) after the word catch does not have a declared type, and may be omitted.

In more detail, here is the syntax:

```
try {
  statements
}
catch (variable) {
  statements
}
finally {
  statements
}
```

Either the catch part or the finally part, but not both, may be omitted.

Execution is as follows:

1. The code in the try block is executed.

   - If no exception occurs, the catch block is skipped.

   - If an exception occurs, control goes immediately to the catch part. The optional *variable* holds a value supplied by the exception; it is a local variable of the catch part.

2. Whether or not an exception occurred, the finally part is executed.

For example, the following code will put up an alert box containing the words "I am an exception":

```
try {
  throw "I am an exception";
```

```
  }
  catch (v) {
    alert(v);
  }
```

Many things that would throw an exception in other languages do not throw an exception in JavaScript. In particular, arithmetic expressions never throw an exception.

A minor complexity arises because JavaScript guarantees that the finally part, if present, will *always* be executed. If the code in the try or catch part tries to execute a return, break, or continue statement, control will pass immediately to finally part, and the return, break, or continue statement will be postponed until after the finally part has finished.

It is also possible for an exception to occur in either the catch or the finally parts of a try-catch-finally statement. The new exception will replace the one being handled and will be treated as a new exception.

2.9.5.5 The with Statement
The with statement is not allowed in strict mode, but you may see it in older code.

```
with object {
  statements
}
```

This uses the *object* as the default prefix for variables; that is, any variable *var* within the statements is treated as *object.var*, wherever this makes sense.

2.10 EXAMPLE: PRIME NUMBERS

Here is a simple program to print all the prime numbers from 2 to 100, properly embedded in an HTML page. This can be saved in a file with the .html extension and viewed in a browser.

```
<!DOCTYPE html>
<html>
<title>Using JavaScript</title>
<head>
<script>
  function isPrime(n) {
    let divisor = 2;
    while (divisor * divisor <= n) {
      if (n % divisor == 0) {
        return false;
      }
      divisor += 1;
    }
    return true;
  }
  </script>
</head>

<body>
Here are some prime numbers:
<script>
  for (let n = 2; n <= 100; n = n + 1) {
    if (isPrime(n)) {
      console(n);
    }
  }
</script>
</body>
</html>
```

There is a problem with the above code; if called with 1, the isPrime function returns true, indicating that 1 is a prime number (it is not). Correcting this is left as an exercise for the reader.

2.11 TESTING

2.11.1 The Mocha Test Framework

Thorough testing results in better code and a good testing framework can make testing relatively painless. Together, **Mocha** and

Chai provide a useful testing framework for JavaScript. Here we present a very brief introduction for using these tools in testing code on an HTML page.

In the <head> section, use the following to load Mocha:

```
<script src="https://cdnjs.cloudflare.com/ajax/libs/
mocha/8.0.1/mocha.js"></script>
```

The following line isn't absolutely necessary, but will provide much neater output:

```
<link rel="stylesheet" href="https://cdnjs.cloudflare.com/
ajax/libs/mocha/8.0.1/mocha.css">
```

The following is one simple way to initialize Mocha:

```
  <script> mocha.setup('bdd'); </script>
```

Use the following to load Chai:

```
<script src="https://cdnjs.cloudflare.com/ajax/libs/
chai/4.2.0/chai.js"></script>
```

The above URLs are long and don't fit on a single line in this book, but you should write them in a single line in your code. Also, these are current versions of Mocha and Chai as I write this, but you may wish to use more recent versions.

We'll talk about the actual tests in the next section. The tests can be put anywhere on the page, or they can be on a separate .js file. We will use the latter approach.

There are two things to put in the body. First, you need the following line to specify where on the page to put the test results:

```
<div id="mocha"></div>
```

The final step, which should be at or near the bottom of the HTML body, is code to run the tests:

```
<script> mocha.run(); </script>
```

2.11.2 Testing with Chai

Very roughly, Mocha is the testing framework, while Chai provides the actual tests. If you are familiar with testing styles, Chai supports the assert, should, and expect styles. We will use the assert style.

A test looks like this:

```
describe(title, function() {
  it("English_description_of_what_it_does", function() {
    // tests go here
  });
});
```

Here are a few of the most useful tests in the chai object. They should be relatively self-explanatory.

- assert(*expression*)

- assert.isTrue(*expression*)

  - Same as assert(*expression*)

- assert.isFalse(*expression*)

- assert.equal(*actual*, *expected*)

  - Usually the *actual* is a function call, and the *expected* is what the function should return.

- assert.notEqual(*actual*, *expected*)

- assert.strictEqual(*actual*, *expected*)

- assert.notStrictEqual(*actual*, *expected*)

- assert.approximately(*actual*, *expected*, *delta*)

- The **delta** is how close two numbers should be, for example, 0.001.

- assert.deepEqual(**actual**, **expected**)

  - Checks the contents of objects, not just identity

All of the above may take a **message** as an additional parameter. This is useful only if there is helpful information to provide.

2.11.3 Testing Example

We previously showed an example JavaScript function to test whether a number is prime. We repeat that example here. For brevity, the code used to print results has been removed. HTML comments, using the <!-- **comment** --> syntax, are used to point out the relevant portions.

```
<!DOCTYPE html>
<html>
<head>
  <title>Testing primes with Mocha and Chai</title>

  <!-- Load Mocha, Chai, and some CSS formatting -->
  <link rel="stylesheet" href="https://cdnjs.
    cloudflare.com/ajax/libs/mocha/8.0.1/mocha.css">
  <script src="https://cdnjs.cloudflare.com/ajax/
    libs/mocha/8.0.1/mocha.js">
    </script>
  <script>mocha.setup('bdd');</script>
  <script src="https://cdnjs.cloudflare.com/ajax/
    libs/chai/4.2.0/chai.js">
    </script>

  <!-- The function to be tested -->
  <script>
    function isPrime(n) {
      let divisor = 2;
      while (divisor <= n / divisor) {
```

```
        if (n % divisor == 0) {
          return false;
        }
        divisor += 1;
      }
      return true;
    }
  </script>

  <!-- The test code; here we load it from a file
    -->
  <script
    src='isPrimeMochaTest.js'>
  </script>

</head>
<body>
  This text goes before the results.

  <!-- The test results will be displayed here -->
  <div id="mocha"></div>

  This text goes after the results.

  <!-- Run the tests and put the result in the
    "mocha" div -->
  <script>
    mocha.run();
  </script>

</body>
</html>
```

The test code can be put directly in the HTML page or loaded from a file. In the above, the test code is on a file named isPrime-MochaTest.js. The contents of that file are as follows:

```
describe("isPrime", function() {
  let assert = chai.assert;
```

```
    it("Tests if n is a prime number", function() {
      assert(isPrime(2));
      assert.isTrue(isPrime(3));
      let x = 4;
      assert.isFalse(isPrime(x));
      assert.equal(isPrime(5), true);
    });
  });
```

(Remember that <script> tags are not used in a .js file.). For the sake of example, several of the possible assert tests are used, and an extra let statement is thrown in to demonstrate that ordinary JavaScript code, not just assertions, can be included.

If all goes well, two results are expected. In the top right corner of the HTML page (put there by the CSS file) should be something like

passes: 1   failures: 0   duration: 0.00s   100%

and at the location of the "mocha" div you should see

```
    isPrime
      √ Tests if n is a prime number
```

CHAPTER 3

JavaScript

In More Detail

JavaScript is a large, complex, and constantly evolving language. The preceding sections have been a whirlwind tour of its main features. What is missing, however, is anything about making interactive web pages—and that, after all, is the main reason to use JavaScript.

If you are eager to get to client-side JavaScript programming, you should now know enough to jump ahead to Chapter 4. If you prefer to deepen your knowledge of JavaScript, continue reading.

3.1 STRICT MODE

No language is perfect. JavaScript allows some things that, in retrospect, should not have been allowed. JavaScript now has a *strict mode* to disallow those features and to modify others. To turn strict mode on globally, put the string

```
"use strict";
```

as the *first* thing in a script; to turn strict mode on for just one function, put that string as the first line inside the function.

DOI: 10.1201/9781003359609-3

Turning on strict mode makes the following things illegal:

- Assigning to a variable that has not been declared with var, let, or const.

- The with statement.

- Defining a function within a conditional or a loop statement.

- Using eval to create variables.

- Using delete to delete a variable, object, function, or an undeletable property (such as prototype).

- Modifying a read-only or get-only property.

- Using eval, with, or any of the reserved keywords as variable names.

- Writing a number with a leading 0 to make it octal, for example, 077.

- Octal escape sequences (other than "\0" to represent the NUL character, which is still allowed).

- Duplicate parameter names in a function, for instance, function foo(a, a).

- Accessing the caller, callee, and arguments properties of functions.

In strict mode, the keyword this inside a function refers to the object that called the function.

> **Caution**: Turning on strict mode *within a function* makes it illegal for that function to have default parameters, a rest parameter, or parameter destructuring.

3.2 IDENTIFIERS

Identifiers consist of letters (as defined by Unicode), digits, underscores, and/or dollar signs; the first character may not be a digit. By convention, the names of variables, properties, functions, and methods should begin with a lowercase letter; names of constructors should begin with a capital letter. Names may be any length.

Case is significant in JavaScript *but not in HTML*. Since JavaScript names are frequently used in HTML, this can lead to some strange errors if you are not careful about case.

As in most other languages, you cannot use a reserved word as an identifier.

3.3 DESTRUCTURING

Destructuring is a way to assign the parts of an object or array into several different variables.

As an example, we use the following object:

```
let p = { givenName: "Sally",
          familyName: "Willis",
          occupation: "doctor" };
```

We may wish to assign the parts of this object into separate variables, as

```
let givenName = p.givenName;
let familyName = p.familyName;
let occupation = p.occupation;
```

Destructuring is a shorter way to do exactly the same thing:

```
let {givenName, familyName, occupation} = p;
```

Property names need not be given in order, and not every name has to be mentioned. Property names that are not actually part of the object may be given; they will receive the value undefined.

To work with a similar object of the same type, say p2, you cannot use let again because variables may only be declared once.

```
let {givenName, familyName, occupation} = p2;
// SyntaxError: Identifier 'givenName' has
// already been declared
```

Neither can you simply omit the word let because starting with an open brace, {, indicates a block.

```
{givenName, familyName, occupation} = p2;
// SyntaxError: Unexpected token '='
```

The solution is to enclose the entire statement, up the semicolon, in parentheses.

```
({givenName, familyName, occupation} = p2);
```

An object may be destructured into different variable names.

```
let {familyName: name, occupation: occ} = p;
// name = "Willis", occ = "doctor"
```

Default values may be given, in case the object lacks the given properties.

```
({givenName: name, country = "USA"} = p);
// name = "Sally", country = "USA"
```

Renaming and giving default values may be combined.

```
({givenName: name="Joe", age=40} = p);
// name = "Sally", age = 40
```

When a function is called, values are assigned to its parameters, and these act like assignment statements; therefore, destructuring may also be used in the parameter list.

```
function f({familyName, occupation: occ,
            age=40, gender: g="male"}) {
```

```
    // When called with f(p), familyName =
    // "Willis", occ = "doctor", age = 40,
    // and g = "male"
}
```

Destructuring may also be used with arrays. Commas are used to indicate array elements that are skipped over.

```
let a = [11, 22, 33, 44];
let [, x, , y] = a;
// x = 22, y = 44
```

3.4 DATA TYPES

3.4.1 Numbers

A *number* may be written as an integer or as a real number. However written, numbers (other than bigints) are stored as double precision floating point numbers and follow the *IEEE Standard for Floating-Point Arithmetic* (*IEEE 754*).

To improve readability, numbers may include underscores, for example, one million may be written as 1_000_000.

Caution: The methods to convert strings to numbers (Number, parseInt, and parseFloat) cannot yet recognize underscores in numbers.

There are some special predefined "numbers":

- NaN ("**N**ot **a N**umber") is the result of expressions such as 0/0 and "one"/"two".

  - You can write this as Number.NaN, or just NaN.

  - Despite the name, NaN *is* a number, and typeof(NaN) will return "number".

  - Arithmetic involving NaN results in NaN.

- Infinity is the result of expressions such as 1/0.

- -Infinity is the result of expressions such as -1/0.

  - isFinite(x) will return false for -Infinity, Infinity, and NaN.

- Number.MIN_VALUE is the smallest number that can be represented, approximately 5e-324.

- Number.EPSILON is approximately 2.220446049250313e-16. It is the smallest number that, when added to one, gives a result different from one.

- Number.MAX_VALUE is the largest number that can be represented, approximately 1.7976931348623157e+308.

- Number.MAX_SAFE_INTEGER is 9007199254740991 ; it is the largest integer that can be uniquely represented as a double precision floating point number.

- Number.MIN_SAFE_INTEGER is -9007199254740991.

All of the above are considered to be numbers. No arithmetic expression will ever cause an exception.

> **Caution**: The function isNaN($value$) returns true if $value$ is NaN, but it also returns true for any $value$ that cannot be converted to a number. To test if the value of variable v really *is* NaN, use the test v != v. This works because NaN is the only value that is not equal to itself.

Some additional methods are Number.isInteger(n), Number.isSafeInteger(n), and Number.isFinite(n).

A *bigint* is an integer written with an n suffix, for example, 123n. Bigints can have an arbitrary number of digits. All the usual numeric operations are available on bigints, except for unary plus: +123n is illegal.

Bigints and (ordinary) numbers cannot be mixed in an arithmetic expression, but bigints and numbers can be compared (using <, <=, etc.). To convert between the two types, use BigInt(*number*) and Number(*bigint*).

A *hexadecimal literal* begins with 0x or 0X. An *octal literal* begins with 0o or 0O.

In strict mode, it is illegal to write a number with a leading zero (e.g. 0123), except for zero itself. In nonstrict mode, some implementations will treat such numbers as octal and others will treat them as decimal.

3.4.2 Strings

A *string* is a sequence of zero or more UTF-16 characters enclosed in either single quotes ('hello'), double quotes ("hello"), or backticks (`hello`). UTF-32 is not supported.

Quote marks of one type may be used within a string enclosed by a different type of quote mark, for example, "Don't go.". Quote marks of the same type as the enclosing type must be escaped (see below).

Strings enclosed in backticks are special. They may span several lines, and anywhere in the string that ${*expression*} occurs, the *expression* is evaluated and becomes part of the string. Strings like this are called *template literals*.

There is no "character" data type. Some characters that cannot be written directly in a string can be "escaped," that is, specified by a backslash followed by a letter or hex number. Characters written in this way still count as single characters.

Escaped characters are:

- \0 NUL
- \b backspace

- \f form feed

- \n newline

- \r carriage return

- \t horizontal tab

- \v vertical tab

- \\ backslash

- \' single quote

- \" double quote

- \` backtick

- \x*DD* Unicode hex *DD*

- \x*DDDD* Unicode hex *DDDD*

The length property of a string is the number of characters in it. Escaped characters, although written with more than one character, still count as a single character; so "abc\n".length is 4.

Strings can be indexed, so *string*[*n*] is the *n*th character in string. However, strings are *immutable*, so you cannot assign a new value to *string*[*n*].

The comparisons <, <=, ==, !=, ===, !==, >=, > can be used with strings. The comparison is according to the Unicode values of the letters, with all uppercase letters preceding (less than) all lowercase letters.

A number of string methods are given in Appendix C.

3.4.3 Booleans

A *boolean* has one of two values: true or false.

JavaScript also has "*truthy*" and "*falsy*" values. When used as a test, the following values are considered false:

- 0 and 0.0
- The empty string, "" or " or ``
- undefined
- null
- NaN

While this feature can be convenient, it makes code less readable.

Older code may use ~n as a test; it is equivalent to n != −1.

3.4.4 Symbols

A *symbol* can be created with or without a description:

```
let sym1 = Symbol();
let sym2 = Symbol("secret");
```

A symbol is a unique identifier; it cannot be confused with any other identifier. Two symbols created with the same description are still different from each other.

Objects have properties, and those properties can be modified or added to. Suppose you have an object that is not one you created—it may be a built-in object, or one from someone else's code—and you want to add a property to it. The property is strictly for your own use; its existence should not affect anyone else's code. The solution is to use a symbol as the property name.

Alternatively, suppose you have an object, and you want to add *meta-information* to the object—that is, information that is *about* the object, but isn't *part of* the object. Again, use a symbol as the property name.

Here is a short map of distances from the sun for various planets:

```
let sun_dist = {"Venus": 108.2, "Earth": 149.6, "Mars":
  227.9};
```

The distances happen to be in millions of kilometers, but that may not be obvious. Let's add that information.

```
let unit = Symbol("mkm");
sun_dist[unit] = "millions of kilometers";
```

We can recover that information by asking for sun_dist[unit], but it is not visible to most code. In particular, the for/in loop will skip right over it.

```
for (let e in sun_dist) {
  console.log(e + " = " + sun_dist[e]);
}
```

will print
```
Venus = 108.2
Earth = 149.6
Mars = 227.9
```

When a string is needed, for example for printing, JavaScript will automatically convert almost anything into its string representation. It does not do this for symbols. To get a string representation of a symbol, you have to explicitly call the toString() method.

```
console.log(unit.toString());
```

will print
```
"Symbol(mkm)"
```

If a symbol is defined with a description, that description is saved in a field named description. For example,

```
console.log(sym2.description);
```

will print
```
"secret"
```

3.4.5 Arrays

Arrays in JavaScript do not have a fixed size; elements may be added to or removed from either end of the array.

- *array*.push(*elems*)—Returns the new length of *array* after adding *elems* to the end.

- *array*.pop()—Removes and returns the last element in *array* and updates its length.

- *array*.unshift(*elems*)—Returns the new length of *array* after adding *elems* to the beginning of *array*.

- *array*.shift()—Removes and returns the first element in *array* and updates the array's length.

The push and pop operations may be used to implement stacks efficiently.

The pairs push and shift, or pop and unshift, may be used to implement queues; all four methods together may be used to implement deques.

Because the unshift and shift methods actually move the elements in the array, they are much less efficient than push and pop.

Several additional array methods are described in Appendix A.

3.4.6 Sparse Arrays

In most languages, arrays are *dense*: an array of size *n* takes up *n* consecutive memory locations. Arrays in JavaScript may be either dense or sparse.

A *sparse array* is one in which only locations containing actual values take up memory in the computer; all other locations appear to contain the special value undefined. Sparse arrays occupy less memory but take more time to process.

Here are some ways to make a sparse array:

- Use the form Array(*length*) to create the array.

- Use delete *array*[*i*] to delete some existing element of *array*.

- Assign a value to *array*[*i*], where *i* > *array*.length.

  - Assigning a value to *array*[*array*.length] does not force the array to be sparse.

- Set the length property of an array to a larger value.

  - If you set length to a smaller value, array elements at that index and beyond are discarded.

- Write a literal array using consecutive commas, for example, ["cat",, "dog",,,].

  - The length of this array is five (not six); the last comma is taken as a trailing comma.

To better understand sparse arrays, it helps to remember that undefined is an actual value in JavaScript, and as such takes up actual space in memory. But if we ask for the value in some location of a sparse array and get undefined, this could mean either (1) there is nothing in that location, or (2) the location really does contain the value undefined.

This has some practical implications. The for/in loop will loop through all indices of an array, whether there is something at that location or not. The for/of loop will only loop through actual values (some of which may be undefined).

The method *array*.hasOwnProperty(*i*) will return true if *array*[*i*] contains an actual value, false if it doesn't.

3.4.7 Sets

JavaScript does not supply the usual operations on sets (union, intersection, difference, symmetric difference). Using the *spread operator* (...), which turns an array into a sequence of values, these operations can be implemented as follows.

```javascript
function union(a, b) {
  return new Set([...a, ...b]);
}

function intersection(a, b) {
  return new Set([...a].filter(x => b.has(x)));
}

function difference(a, b) {
  return new Set([...a].filter(x => !b.has(x)));
}

function symmetricDifference(a, b) {
  return difference(union(a, b), intersection(a, b));
}
```

3.4.8 Maps

In many languages, it is undesirable to use mutable objects as keys. This is not an issue in JavaScript, which compares keys for identity rather than equality. No matter what changes are made to an object used as a key, it retains its identity; a different "equal" object cannot be used to recover the associated value.

> **Caution**: Every object literal is a unique object. If you use an object literal as a key, you will never be able to "recreate" that key. You can, however, iterate over the map.

Three new methods have recently been added to Maps:

- *map*.keys()—Returns an iterator for the keys of *map*.

- *map*.values()—Returns an iterator for the values in *map*.

- *map*.entries()—Returns an iterator for the entries of *map*, where each entry is returned as a [*key, value*] array.

The for(let *var* of *iterator*) {...} loop is the easiest way to use an iterator.

3.4.9 WeakMaps

JavaScript uses **automatic garbage collection**: Space is allocated for objects when needed, and reclaimed when those objects become inaccessible. Objects become inaccessible when the program no longer has any way to refer to them.

As a trivial example,

```
let car = {make: "Suburu", year: 2018};
car = {make: "Toyota", color: "white"};
```

After the second assignment, there is no longer any way to access the object {make: "Suburu", year: 2018}, therefore it can be garbage collected.

A WeakMap is like a Map—it matches keys to values. Here are the differences:

- The constructor is WeakMap().

- Only objects, not primitives, can be used as keys.

- Only the methods get(*key*), set(*key, value*), has(*key*), and delete(*value*) are provided.

- WeakMaps are not iterable, so you cannot use for/of with them.

A key that is in a Map can never be garbage collected; but a key in a WeakMap can be garbage collected (and the entry deleted from the WeakMap) if there are no other references to it.

This last is the most important point. Objects that have only a temporary existence can be used as keys in a WeakMap, thus allowing garbage collection to do its job.

Garbage collection can happen at unpredictable times. Consequently, the state of a WeakMap at any given time may be nondeterministic. The only allowable methods on a WeakMap are those for which this will not be an issue.

3.4.10 Promises

If you have a long-running task whose results are not needed immediately, such as a file transfer, you may wish to start it running asynchronously while your code continues to do other things. A *promise* is code that runs asynchronously and "promises" to complete a task at some later time.

The following assignment statement creates a Promise object, saves it in *promise*, and starts the *function* executing:

```
let promise = new Promise(function);
```

> **Caution**: Keep in mind the distinction between a *function* and a *function call*. If we define function f(){}, then f is the function itself, while f() is a call to that function. The argument to the Promise constructor must be a function.

There are three ways a promise can terminate: By reporting "success," by reporting "failure," or by throwing an exception. To deal with this, the *function* used by the promise should have two parameters, each of which is also a function (sometimes called a *callback*). The promise code should call the first function to report success, or the second to report failure.

It is often convenient to use *arrow functions* (described later) to write the callback functions of a promise. Like this:

```
new Promise((onSuccess, onFailure) => {code});
```

In this syntax, *code* is the (possibly long-running) code to be executed, *onSuccess* is a function to execute if *code* is successful, and *onFailure* is a function to execute if the code fails. Note especially that the arguments given to the parameters *onSuccess* and *onFailure* must be functions; each of these functions may take one argument, or none.

The promise's then method supplies the functions for the promise to use.

- *promise*.then(*successFunction*, *failureFunction*)—Tells the promise which function to call upon success or failure.

  - Calling either *successFunction* or *failureFunction* will terminate the promise.

  - If an unhandled exception occurs, the *failureFunction* is called.

The following example uses three functions: yes and no just print their argument, while doSomething chooses a random number and "succeeds" if the number is greater than 0.5, or throws an exception if the number is smaller. (For simplicity, the example uses Math.random instead of some task that might actually take a long time.)

```
function yes(r) {
  console.log("yes, " + r);
}

function no(e) {
  console.log("no, " + e);
}

function doSomething(resolve, reject) {
  let r = Math.random();
  if (r > 0.50) resolve(r); // succeed
  throw r + " is too low";  // fail
}
```

Here we make use of those functions:

```
let promise = new Promise(doSomething);
// other work
promise.then(yes, no);
console.log("END");
```

Example results:

```
"END"
"no, 0.18252962330109224 is too low"

"END"
"yes, 0.938714265780423"
```

The result returned by then is a Promise. This allows promises to be "chained," so that the value returned by then can be fed into another then. The following example will create a random number, then multiply it by 100, then add 1000, then display the result.

```
let promise2 = new Promise(
  someFun => { return someFun(Math.random());
  }).then(function(result) { return 100 * result;
  }).then(function(result) { return 1000 + result;
  }).then(function(result) { console.log(result);
  });
```

The syntax does not allow extra arguments to be passed to a Promise; any additional information it needs must be taken from the environment.

3.4.11 Conversions

JavaScript performs most conversions (coercions) automatically. You can also do explicit conversions with the functions Number(*x*), String(*x*), Boolean(*x*), BigInt(*x*), parseInt(*x*, *base*), and parseFloat(*x*).

Caution: If you use the word new with one of the functions Number, String, or Boolean, the result will be a "wrapper object," that is, an object containing the value, *not* a value of the named type. This will mostly continue to work (except for a Boolean object, which is always "truthy").

All objects have a toString method, which can be called as *object*. toString(). It is usually a good idea to override this method for your own objects.

The following functions convert between strings and numbers:

- Number(*string*)—Converts the entire *string* into a number, if possible, otherwise it returns NaN (**Not a N**umber).

- parseInt(*string*)—Converts the initial characters of *string* into a number, if possible, otherwise it returns NaN. ParseInt ignores any following characters that do not belong in an integer, such as a decimal point.

- parseFloat(*string*)—Converts the initial characters of *string* into a number, if possible, otherwise it returns NaN. parseFloat ignores any following characters that do not belong in a number.

- *variable*.toFixed(*d*)—Converts the number in *variable* to a string with *d* digits after the decimal point.

- *variable*.toString(*base*)—Converts the number in *variable* to a string representation of that number in the given *base* (2 to 36).

For both toFixed and toString, if a literal integer is used in place of the *variable*, two dots are required—one as part of the number, the second to indicate a method call (for example, 123.. toString(8) or 123.0.toString(8)).

Conversions can be made between plain objects, maps, and arrays of two-element arrays.

- *array* = `Array.from(`*map*`)`;

- *array* = `Object.entries(`*object*`)`;

- *map* = `new Map(`*array*`)`;

- *map* = `new Map(Object.entries(`*object*`))`;

- *object* = `Object.fromEntries(`*map*`)`;

- *object* = `Object.fromEntries(`*array*`)`;

3.5 MATH

The Math class supplies the constants `Math.E` (e), `Math.PI` (π), `Math.LN2` ($\log_e 2$), and `Math.LN10` ($\log_e 10$), among others.

Some of the methods supplied by the Math class are:

- `Math.abs(`*x*`)` — Returns the absolute value of *x*.

- `Math.sign(`*x*`)` — Returns the one of -1, 0, or 1 that has the same sign as *x*.

- `Math.trunc(`*x*`)` — Returns the integer portion of *x*.

- `Math.round(`*x*`)` — Returns the integer nearest to *x*.

- `Math.floor(`*x*`)` — Returns the largest integer less than or equal to *x*.

- `Math.ceil(`*x*`)` — Returns the smallest integer greater than or equal to *x*.

- `Math.max(`*x1*, *x2*, ..., *xN*`)` — Returns the largest of its arguments.

- `Math.min(`*x1*, *x2*, ..., *xN*`)` — Returns the smallest of its arguments.

- `Math.sqrt(x)` — Returns the positive square root of *x*.

- `Math.cbrt(x)` — Returns the cube root of *x*.

- `Math.random()` — Returns a pseudo-random number *r* in the range $0 <= r < 1$.

The Math class also supplies the standard logarithmic and trigno-metric functions `exp`, `log`, `log10`, `log2`, `sin`, `cos`, `tan`, `asin`, `acos`, `atan`, as well as the hyperbolic functions `sinh`, `cosh`, `tanh`, `asinh`, `acosh`, and `atanh`. All angles are in radians.

3.6 RESERVED WORDS

Most languages have a set of *reserved words*, or *keywords*, that have special meaning and that cannot be used for identifiers.

JavaScript is unusual in that the set of reserved words keeps changing. It was defined with more reserved words than were actually used, to allow for future expansion. Subsequently some new words were reserved, and some were unreserved. Table 3.1 should be a reasonably current list.

TABLE 3.1 JavaScript Keywords

arguments	else	in	super
await	enum	instanceof	switch
break	eval	interface	this
case	export	let	throw
catch	extends	new	true
class	false	null	try
const	finally	package	typeof
continue	for	private	var
debugger	function	protected	void
default	if	public	while
delete	implements	return	with
do	import	static	yield

You should avoid using the following as identifiers:

- Words that are no longer reserved: abstract, boolean, byte, char, double, final, float, goto, int, long, native, short, synchronized, throws, transient, and volatile.

- The names of JavaScript objects, properties, and methods, such as Array.

- The names of HTML objects and properties, such as button.

- The names of HTML event handlers, such as onkeypress.

3.7 GOOD OPERATORS

An *expression* is any JavaScript code that results in a value. Expressions may be as simple as a single constant or single variable.

Operators with higher *precedence* (indicated by larger numbers) are performed before those with lower precedence. For example, in the expression 2 * 3 + 4 * 5, the multiplications are done before the addition because multiplication has higher precedence than addition. A number of things not often thought of as operators, for example parentheses and array indexing, also have precedence.

When operators have equal precedence, their *associativity* ("left to right" or "right to left") determines which operations are done first. For example, subtraction is *left associative*, so 10 - 5 - 3 means (10 - 5) - 3 rather than 10 - (5 - 3). Almost all binary operators (except exponentiation) are left associative; the assignment operators are *right associative*, so a = b = c + 5 means a = (b = c + 5) rather than (a = b) = c + 5.

Parentheses can be used to override the above rules and specify an explicit order of evaluation. Parentheses are also used to show the order of evaluation when it might not be obvious.

Table 3.2 lists the most important operators. The meaning of many of them should be obvious; the less common operators will be explained as needed.

TABLE 3.2 JavaScript's "Good" Operators

Operator	Purpose	Associativity	Precedence
( )	Grouping	n/a	21
obj . *prop*	Property access	Left	20
ary[*index*]	Index into array	Left	20
new *type*(*args*)	Object creation	n/a	20
fun(*args*)	Function call	Left	20
obj ?. *prop*	Optional chaining	Left	20
new *type*	Object creation	Right	19
! *value*	Logical NOT	Right	17
+ *value*	Unary plus	Right	17
- *value*	Unary minus	Right	17
typeof *value*	Type (as string)	Right	17
void *value*	Treat as undefined	Right	17
delete *obj*.*prop*	Remove property	Right	17
expr ** *expr*	Exponentiation	Right	16
expr * *expr*	Multiplication	Left	15
expr / *expr*	Division	Left	15
expr % *expr*	Remainder	Left	15
expr + *expr*	Addition	Left	14
expr - *expr*	Subtraction	Left	14
expr < *expr*	Less than	Left	12
expr <= *expr*	Less or equal	Left	12
expr > *expr*	Greater than	Left	12
expr >= *expr*	Greater or equal	Left	12
expr in *expr*	Object has property	Left	12
expr instanceof *type*	Object is type	Left	12
expr == *expr*	Is equal to	Left	11
expr != *expr*	Is not equal to	Left	11
expr === *expr*	Strictly equal	Left	11
expr !== *expr*	Not strictly equal	Left	11
expr && *expr*	Logical AND	Left	6

(Continued)

TABLE 3.2 *(Continued)*   JavaScript's "Good" Operators

Operator	Purpose	Associativity	Precedence
expr || *expr*	Logical OR	Left	5
test ? *expr* : *expr*	If-then-else	Right	4
id = *expr*	Simple assignment	Right	3
id op expr, where *op* is one of **= *= /= %= += -=&&= ||= ??=	Stands for *id* = *id op expr*	Right	3
yield *expr*	Coroutine exit	Right	2
expr , *expr*	Multiple evaluation	Left	1

3.8 OPERATOR NOTES

The && operator means "and." The \|\| operator means "or."

The logical operators && and \|\| are *short-circuit* operators. That is, if the result is known from the first (left-hand) expression, the second (right-hand) expression is not evaluated. Because JavaScript has "truthy" and "falsy" values, the && and \|\| operators don't necessarily return either true or false, but may instead return a truthy or falsy value.

- *expr1* && *expr2*—If *expr1* is falsy, the result is *expr1*, else the result is *expr2*.

- *expr1* \|\| *expr2*—If *expr1* is truthy, the result is *expr1*, else the result is *expr2*.

Given a sequence of values connected with &&, the result is either the first falsy value encountered, or the final truthy value. Similarly, given a sequence of values connected with \|\|, the result is either the first truthy value encountered, or the final falsy value. This fact is sometimes used in a "clever" way; for example, the expression x \|\| 5 has the value 5 if x is zero (or some other falsy value), otherwise it has the value of x.

The various assignment operators *are* operators; that is, they have a value and may be embedded in a larger expression, for example, y = 3 + (x += 5).

The void *expression* operator evaluates *expression* but returns the value undefined.

The ***nullish coalescing operator***, ??, has the value of its left operand if that operand is not null or undefined, otherwise it has the value of its right operand. It behaves a lot like || —given a sequence of values connected with ??, the result is either the first "defined" (neither null nor undefined) value, or the final value.

&& has a higher precedence than ||, and both have a higher precedence than ??.

> **Note**: When ?? is used in an expression with either && or
> ||, parentheses *must* be used to show the desired order of
> operations.

3.9 BAD OPERATORS

In his excellent book *JavaScript: The Good Parts*, Douglas Crockford made the case that there are features of JavaScript that should not be used. We mention a number of these, with brief explanations, in Table 3.3.

When used as a prefix, ++ adds one to its operand before using the value of the operand in an expression. When used as a suffix, ++ uses the original value of the operand in the enclosing expression, and adds one to the operand afterward. Similar remarks hold for the -- operator. These operators should only be used as complete statements, or as the increment part of a for loop; other expressions are too confusing. For example, the statement x = x++ does nothing. As complete statements, x += 1 is at least as clear as x++ and doesn't require that many more keystrokes.

The ***bitwise operators*** (&, |, ^, ~, >>, >>>, <<) convert their operands to 32-bit integers—a data type that JavaScript supposedly does not have—perform the operation, and convert back. This works, but is slow.

TABLE 3.3   JavaScript's "Bad" Operators

Operator	Purpose	Associativity	Precedence
id ++	Postfix increment	n/a	18
id --	Postfix decrement	n/a	18
++ *id*	Prefix increment	Right	17
-- *id*	Prefix decrement	Right	17
expr << *shift*	Left shift zero fill	Left	13
expr >> *shift*	Right shift sign fill	Left	13
expr >>> *shift*	Right shift zero fill	Left	13
expr == *expr*	Is equal to	Left	11
expr != *expr*	Is not equal to	Left	11
expo & *expr*	Bitwise AND	Left	10
expr ^ *expr*	Bitwise exclusive OR	Left	9
expr | *expr*	Bitwise OR	Left	8
id op expr, where *op* is one of &= ^= |= <<= >>= >>>=	*id* = *id op expr*	Right	3

The reader may have noticed that the comparison operators == and != are in both the "good" and the "bad" tables. It is fine to use these operators with values of the same type. If the operands of == or != are of different types, JavaScript first tries to convert them to the same type. In most cases this works, but the rules are complex and confusing. The operators === and !== do no type conversion, so values of different types are unequal.

3.10 FUNCTIONS

3.10.1 Defining Functions

JavaScript provides several ways to define functions. As an example, the function square may be defined in any of these ways:

- `function square(x) { return x * x; }`

  - This is a *function statement*.

- `let square = new Function("x", "return x * x");`

- This uses the Function() **constructor**. The arguments to the function are given as strings, and the final string is the function body.

- `let square = function(x) { return x * x; }`

  - The part following the equals sign is a **function literal**.

- `let square = function sqr(x) { return x * x; }`

  - This is a **named function literal**. The scope of the name sqr is the function block, so it is available *only* within the function body, where it can be used to invoke the function recursively.

- `let square = (x) => x * x;`

  - This is an **arrow function**. If there is only one parameter, the parentheses may be omitted. The single expression after the arrow is the result.

- `let square = (x) => { return x * x; }`

  - This is another **arrow function**, showing that braces may be used, in which case the return statement is needed.

All functions have a name property.

- If the function is created using the Function constructor, the name is "anonymous".

- If a name immediately follows the word function, that is the name of the function.

- If an unnamed function is immediately assigned to a variable, that variable becomes the name of the function.

- Otherwise, the name of the function is the empty string.

Function statements may be defined within other functions, but they should be at the top level of the function, not within another statement such as a loop or if statement. Such functions are local to the enclosing function:

```
function hypotenuse(x, y) {
    function square(x) { return x * x }
    return Math.sqrt(square(x) + square(y));
}
```

Primitive values (number, string, boolean) are passed to a function *by value*; objects are passed *by reference*. What this means is that functions receive a copy of primitive values, so there is nothing that can be done to them that will be seen by the calling program. For objects, functions receive a reference to the actual object; any changes made to the interior of the object will be seen by the calling program.

In other words, changing the value of a parameter within a function does not change the value outside the function, but changing the properties of an object passed as a parameter does change their values outside the function.

3.10.2 Parameters and Arguments

We use the following terminology: A *parameter* is a variable in the head of a function definition; an *argument* is an expression in a call to that function.

JavaScript does not require that a function be called with the same number of arguments as it has parameters. Excess arguments are ignored, while missing arguments have the value undefined.

In a function, the special variable arguments is an array-like object that holds *all* the arguments the function was called with, regardless of how many parameters were used in the function definition. It can be indexed like an array, or looped over with for loops, but lacks most of the other capabilities of an array. The arguments variable is used mostly in older code; it isn't allowed in strict mode. Modern code is more likely to use rest parameters (see below).

Parameters may be given default values; if the argument is missing, the default value is used. Default values have the form of assignments, and previous parameters may be used in the expression. For example,

```javascript
function foo(a, b = 10, c = a * b) {
  return a + b + c;
}
console.log(foo(3)); // result is 43
```

Because arguments are matched to parameters by position (first argument goes to first parameter, etc.), all parameters without default values must precede all parameters with default values.

A **rest parameter** is a parameter that collects all the remaining arguments into an array. A rest parameter is designated by preceding it with three dots (...). For example, if a function is defined with

```javascript
function foo(x, y, ...z) {
  console.log(`x is ${x}`);
  console.log(`y is ${y}`);
  console.log(`z is ${z}`);
}
```

and called with

```javascript
foo(1, 2, 3, 4, 5);
```

then the following is written to the console:

```
"x is 1"
"y is 2"
"z is 3,4,5"
```

Since the ... collects all the remaining arguments, it can only be used as the last parameter.

The dots can also be used in reverse, in the arguments to a function. When placed before an array in a function call, the values in the array are separated into individual arguments. This is useful for functions that take an arbitrary number of arguments.

```
let ary = [2, 7, 1, 3];
let m = Math.max(...ary);
```

Used in this way, the dots are called a *spread*. Spreads can also be applied to sets and maps.

Spreads can be used to make shallow copies of arrays.

```
let ary2 = [...ary];
```

3.10.3 Functions Are Data

The name of a function, not followed by an argument list, refers to the function itself. Functions may be assigned to variables:

```
function square(x) {
   return x * x;
}

let square2 = square;
let result = square2(5); // 25

let myArray = new Array();
myArray[10] = square;
result = myArray[10](7); // 49
```

Functions can be printed. The call square.toString() will return a listing of the function, much as it appears above.

Functions may be assigned to properties. A function assigned to a property is called a *method*. Within a method, this refers to the call object, that is, to the object that holds the property.

Functions may be passed as arguments to another function:

```
myArray.sort(function(a,b) { return a - b });
```

In this example, the sort method uses the function to determine how to compare elements of myArray.

3.10.4 Functions Are Objects

Functions are objects, and objects have ***properties***.

The length property of a function is the number of parameters in its definition. A rest parameter (one preceded by ...) is not included in the count.

The name property of a function is, of course, its name. JavaScript is quite clever at determining the name of a function. For example, given the definition

```
let square = (x) => x * x;
```

the function is defined as an anonymous literal function, but the assignment to the variable square is enough to let JavaScript decide that the function is named "square".

Functions may be ***recursive***; that is, they may call themselves. A simple example is computing the factorial function:

```
let factorial = function f(n) {
   if (n == 0) return 1;
   return n * f(n - 1);
};
```

This example uses a ***named function literal***. With this definition, the name f can be used only within the function definition, while the name factorial can be used both inside and outside the function.

Function properties are often a good alternative to global variables. For example,

```
nextInt.counter = 0;
function nextInt() {
  nextInt.counter += 1;
  return nextInt.counter;
}
```

The first call to nextInt will return 1, the second will return 2, and so on because the function changes the value of its counter property. Also, note that because functions are **hoisted** (processed first), the assignment to a function property can occur lexically before the function definition.

3.10.5 Function Methods

A **method** is a function that belongs to an object. But functions themselves are objects, and have methods. Consider:

```
let car = { make: "Subaru", year: 2018,
    age(now) { return now - this.year; } };
let fn = car.age;
```

At this point fn is a function, specifically the function age() {return year - this.year}. It is no longer attached to an object, therefore it is no longer a method. Unfortunately, it still refers to this, which has also lost its attachment to the original object.

There are three methods that can help solve the problem with this.

- *f*.call(***obj***, ***arg1***, ..., ***argN***) — Calls the function or method *f* with the given arguments, using ***obj*** as the value of this. If no object is required, ***obj*** may be null.

  - fn.call(car, 2021) — Returns 3. Note that the function fn can be applied to any object with a year property.

- *f*.apply(*obj*, *args*) — Does the same as call, but expects an array of arguments.

  - fn.apply(car, [2021]) — Returns 3.

- let *g* = *f*.bind(*obj*, *arg1*, ..., *argN*) — Returns a new function *g* that uses *obj* as the value of this, and with the first *N* arguments filled in.

  - let g = fn.bind(car) — Assigns to g a function that expects an argument for the year parameter.

  - let h = bind(car, 2021) — Assigns to h a function that expects no arguments and returns 3.

3.10.6 Closures

Suppose one function is defined inside another; call them the "outer function" and the "inner function." The outer function forms the environment of the inner function, so the inner function can use the local variables of the outer function. If the outer function returns, all its local variables will (normally) be recycled.

But what if the inner function continues to exist after the outer function vanishes? That can happen—the (previously) inner function could be stored in a variable, or perhaps returned as a result of the outer function. If the inner function is executed, it still needs access to the local variables of the outer function.

The solution is that those local variables don't get recycled— they are "closed over" and kept for use of the (previously) inner function.

```
function make_counter() {
    let n = 0;
    let count = function() {
        n += 1;
```

```
      return n;
    }
    return count;
  }

  let counter = make_counter();
  console.log(counter()); // 1
  console.log(counter()); // 2
```

Here the make_counter function declares a local variable n, which is used in the count function. The count function is then returned as a result of make_counter, but it still has access to the storage location used by variable n, which is "closed over" by count. This is termed a *closure*. (The *name* n is recycled and no longer accessible, but the storage it used is not released.)

Each time make_counter is called it creates a *new* local variable n, independent of any previous ones. In this way, multiple independent counters can be created.

It isn't necessary to use nested functions to create closures. A function created in a block, using variables of that block, can be put in a variable with a scope larger than the block. The result is still a closure.

```
  let v; // outside the block
  { let n = 0;
    let count = function() {
      n += 1;
      return n;
    }
    v = count;
  }

  console.log(v()); // 1
  console.log(v()); // 2
```

3.10.7 Generators

A *generator* is a special kind of function that remembers where it is at in the function, and when used again, resumes from where it left off. This is useful for producing a (possibly infinite) sequence of values.

To define a generator:

- Begin with function* rather than function.
- Use yield *value* instead of return *value*. When yield is executed, it returns an object {value: *value*, done: false}.
  - The next use of the generator will resume execution right after the yield statement.
  - Using a return statement, or reaching the end of the function, will terminate the generator; the value returned is the object {value: undefined, done: true}.

To use a generator:

- Call the function defined with function*. This returns a *generator object*, not a value computed by the generator.
- Use the generator object in a for/of loop (*not* for/in, which will do nothing); **or**
- Call the generator's next() method as many times as desired. This returns an object as described above.
  - A generator can only be used once. Once a generator is done, it's done. You can always make a new one, though.

As an example, we will write a very simple generator that takes an argument n and repeatedly cuts it in half, rounding down to the nearest integer, until 1 is returned.

```
function* half(n) {
    yield n;
```

```
    while (n > 1) {
      n = Math.floor(n / 2);
      yield n;
    }
}
```

We can use it like this:

```
    let gen = half(10);
    for (i of gen) {
      console.log(i);
    }
```

This will produce the values 10, 5, 2, and 1.

Alternatively, we can explicitly use the generator's next() method.

```
    gen = half(10);
    let obj = gen.next();
    while (! obj.done) {
      console.log(obj.value);
      obj = gen.next();
    }
```

This will produce the same sequence of values.

3.10.8 Iterators

An *iterable* is any object that can be stepped through, one element after another. An *iterator* is an object that implements a method for stepping through the elements of an iterable. Arrays, sets, maps, and strings are all iterable objects; the for/of statement uses an iterator to step through them.

You can make an iterator for objects you create. The requirements are:

- The object must have a property whose name is the system-defined Symbol.iterator.

- The value of that property must be a method named next, which takes no arguments and returns an object with the fields value and done.

  - If done is true, the iteration ends and value is ignored.

The syntax for creating an iterator can get quite confusing. One simplification is to define the required next() method as a generator, since generators are a kind of function and return the required kind of value.

As an example, we define a range object:

```
let range = {start:10, step: 5, end: 25};
```

Next we will add to this object an iterator that will produce the values start, start+step, and so on, up to but not including end.

```
range[Symbol.iterator] =
  function* next() {
    n = this.start;
    while (n < this.end) {
      yield n;
      n += this.step;
    }
  };
```

and test it:

```
for (let e of range) {
  console.log(e);
}
```

This gives the correct values 10, 15, and 20.

Notice the use of the word this. As mentioned earlier, when this is used in a method (a function belonging to an object), it refers to the containing object.

In the above, an iterator was added to an existing object. It can also be added when an object is created.

```
{start:12, step: 5, end: 30,
  [Symbol.iterator]: function* next() {…} }.
```

3.11 OBJECTS

3.11.1 Definition of Objects

JavaScript is an object-oriented language.

In JavaScript, you can create objects without having to first define a class. This section is about objects; classes will be covered later.

An **object** is a collection of named values (called **properties** or **fields**). Objects use dot notation, as in other object-oriented languages, but they behave more like hash tables (also called maps or dictionaries).

You can write an **object literal** by enclosing **key**:**value** pairs in braces. For example:

```
let car = {make: "Subaru", year: 2018}
```

This defines the object car with the properties make and year. You can refer to the fields with **dot notation**. For example, the statement

```
console.log(car.make + " " + car.year);
```

will write "Subaru 2018" to the console. If you don't have a console open, you won't see the result; in that case you may wish to use

```
alert(car.make + " " + car.year);
```

instead.

We can add properties to an existing object:

```
car.mileage = 25041;
```

or delete them:

```
delete car.mileage;
```

Property names (the "key" part of **key**: **value**) are always either strings (which do not need to be quoted) or symbols. It may not look that way; the following is legal:

```
let nums = {2: "two", 3.1416: "pi"}
```

In this code, the keys are actually the *strings* "2" and "3.1416".

There is a second way to access properties: You can use brackets, [], instead of dot notation. Instead of nums.2 or nums.3.1416, which are illegal syntax, you can say nums[2] and nums[3.1416]. Any expression within the brackets will be evaluated and the result converted to a string; so nums[5-3] is the same as nums["2"].

Brackets can also be used when creating or adding to an object. Continuing the above example, either of the following two statements could be used to add the property mileage to car, or update the value of mileage if it is already a property:

```
car.mileage = 25300;
car["mileage"] = 25300;
```

When creating an object, brackets can be used to compute the name of a property (the key), the value, or both.

```
let property = "make";
let make = "Subaru";
let age = 2;
car = {[property]: [make], year: 2020 - age}
```

If you have some variables containing values and you want to create an object with the same names and values, there is a very convenient shorthand you can use. Writing just a variable name is the same as adding a property with that name and the variable's value. For example, if

```
let make = "Subaru";
let year = 2018;
```
then

```
let car = {make, year}
```

is shorthand for

```
let car = {make: "Subaru", year: 2018}
```

To test whether an object has a particular property, use the in operator. For example, "make" in car returns true.

You can use the for/in loop to step through all the properties of an object. The code

```
for (prop in car) {
    console.log(prop + " is " + car[prop])
}
```

will display the following on the console:

```
"make is Subaru"
"year is 2018"
```

3.11.2 Creating Objects

In the previous section we made an object by writing an object literal, {make: "Subaru", year: 2018}, which we then assigned to the variable car.

Another way to create the car object is to first create a "blank" object, then add properties to it:

```
let car = Object();  // or let car = {};
car.make = "Subaru"; // don't use 'let' here
car.year = 2018;
```

Yet another way to create this object is to write a function that assigns values to properties of the keyword this, then explicitly returns this as a result.

```
function Car(make, year) {
  this.make = make;
  this.year = year;
  return this;
}
```

We can call this function in the usual way.

```
let car = Car("Subaru", 2018);
```

Notice that the function uses the names make and year both as variables and as property names. This is by no means necessary; we could have used different names for the variables as for the properties. But it is convenient to be able to use the same names, rather than having to think up synonyms.

There is yet another way to create a car object. Again we write a function, but this time we do not explicitly return this as a result.

```
function Car(make, year) {
  this.make = make;
  this.year = year;
}
```

Because there is no explicit return statement, this function will return undefined if called in the usual way. Nevertheless, we can use it to get a car object by putting the keyword new in the function call.

```
let car = new Car("Subaru", 2018);
```

Putting new in front of a function call does two things. It creates a new local variable named this inside the function, and it implicitly returns this as a result.

A function used in this way acts as a **constructor** for objects. It is conventional to capitalize the first letter of a constructor (hence, Car rather than car). Constructors are used when it is desirable to define a number of similar objects, for example, a number of car objects.

> **Note:** By default, a constructor returns the newly created object this. A different object, but not a primitive, may be explicitly returned by using the return statement. Attempting to return a primitive value has no effect.

When an object is created by calling a constructor, the test **object** instanceof **constructor** (for example, car instanceof Car) will test whether the object was created using that constructor. This is in contrast to typeof(car), which will return the string "object".

The Object.create(**proto**) method uses an existing object **proto** as the **prototype** for a new object. The newly created object has no properties of its own; it is "transparent," in the sense that any attempt to read its properties will "see through it" and read the properties of the prototype.

```
let car2 = Object.create(car);
car2.make = "VW";
car2.color = "blue";
```

Following these statements, car will be unchanged, but car2 will have "VW" as its make, "blue" as its color, and 2018 as its year.

3.11.3 Copying Objects

As is the case with most languages, a variable holds only a small amount of information, such as a single number. Objects, including arrays, sets, maps, and user-created objects, take up a great deal more room. Consequently, what is actually "in" a variable is a *reference* (or *pointer* or *machine address*), specifying where to find the object.

If obj1 is a variable whose value is an object, then the assignment obj2 = obj1 copies the *reference* into obj2, not the object itself. The result is that obj1 and obj2 both point to the same object. Any changes to that object are equally visible from both variables.

There is no way in JavaScript to directly copy an object. However, there is a way to copy all the properties of an object, or even several objects, into another object

```
let newObj = Object.assign({}, oldObj);
```

The Object.assign method takes an empty object {}, given as the first parameter, and copies all the properties of the second parameter into it, returning the result.

In fact, the assign method is quite general. It can take any number of objects as parameters, and copy the properties of all succeeding objects into the first object. It also returns the first object as a result.

```
Object.assign(newObj, oldObj1, …, oldObjN);
```

If there is a conflict, later values of a property overwrite earlier ones.

This is a *shallow copy*: The keys and values of the properties are copied, but if a value is itself an object, it is the *reference* to that object that is copied, not the object itself.

3.11.4 Methods

A ***method*** is a function attached to an object.

```
let now = new Date().getFullYear();
let car = { make: "Subaru",
            year: 2018,
            age: function() {
                return now - this.year;
            }
        }
```

In the above, new Date() returns a Date object, and its method getFullYear() returns a four-digit number.

The above car object has a property named year. It isn't a variable; you can't just say year, you have to say which object it belongs to. The keyword this means "this same object."

A method inside an object literal can be abbreviated by leaving out the colon and the word function. Within car, age could be defined as follows:

```
age() { return now - this.year; }
```

The parentheses after age are enough to indicate that it is a function.

3.11.5 Optional Chaining

Objects can contain references to other objects. For example, a Customer object might have an address property, while an Address might have a number property.

```
let cust = {
  name: "Jones",
  address: { number: 29, street: "main" }
}
```

With this object you might say cust.address.number. This is an example of *chaining*.

Sometimes information is missing or incomplete. If either cust or cust.address is undefined or null, then cust.address.number will result in an error.

To avoid this error, the *optional chaining operator* ?. can be used. It converts errors into the undefined value. Hence, cust?.address?.number will either work or it will return undefined, but it won't cause an error.

Optional chaining can also be used when:

- Using brackets to access a property: cust?.["address"],
- Indexing into an array: ary?.[n], and
- Calling a possibly undefined method: cust.getOrder?.().
  - This will result in an error if the cust.getOrder property exists but is not a function.

3.11.6 This

> You keep using that word. I do not think it means what you think it means.
> —William Goldman, The Princess Bride

In JavaScript, the keyword this has a number of meanings. The first two given below are the most common uses.

- **In a method** (a function belonging to an object), this refers to the containing object.
  - This is similar to the use of this in Java or C++, or self in Python.

- **In a constructor** (a function called with new), this refers to the object under construction.

- **At the top level** of a program, this refers to the *global object*.

  - In a browser, the global object is the Window object.

- **In a function,**

  - **In nonstrict mode,** this refers to the *global object*. In a browser, the global object is the Window object.

  - **In strict mode,** this has the value undefined.

  - **In a function inside a method,** this has the same meaning it does in a top-level function; it does not refer to the object that owns the method.

- **In an arrow function,** the meaning of this is the same as it would be if it were in the surrounding context (not in the arrow function).

- **In an event handler,** this refers to the HTML element that received the event.

The value of this is defined at run time, not at compile time. For example, the word this may be used in a function, where it initially has the value undefined. Later, that function may be stored as a method of an object, with the result that this refers to the object.

The global object isn't always Window. In Node.js the global object is global, while in Web Workers it is self. For code that will work in any of these environments, use globalThis to refer to the global object.

3.11.7 Higher-Order Functions

A *higher-order function/method* is a function or method that expects a function as one of its arguments. Arrays have a number of higher-order methods. It is common for a function used as an agument to be defined directly in the method call, using the arrow notation. In this section we provide a couple of examples; a more complete list is in Appendix B.

Reminder: An arrow function has the syntax (*parameters*) => *expression*.

The sort method takes a function of two arguments that returns a negative, zero, or positive value if the first argument to that function is less than, equal to, or greater than the second argument, respectively.

```
let nums = [12, 43, 115, 9, 65, 1001, 902];

nums.sort((a, b) => a - b);
// nums is [9, 12, 43, 65, 115, 902, 1001]

nums.sort((a, b) => b - a);
// nums is [1001, 902, 115, 65, 43, 12, 9]

nums.sort((a, b) => a % 10 - b % 10);
// nums is [1001, 902, 12, 43, 115, 65, 9]
```

This last example sorts numbers according to their one's digit (the number modulo 10).

Higher-order methods can be used to replace many kinds of loops, resulting in shorter and more readable code. For example, the map method will apply a function to every element of an array, producing an array of results.

```
a = [1, 2, 3, 4, 5];
asq = a.map(e => e ** 2);
// asq = [1, 4, 9, 16, 25]
```

The filter method removes unwanted values from an array, returning a new, shorter array.

```
a = [87, -1, 92, -1, -1, 98];
afil = a.filter(x => x >= 0);
// afil = [87, 92, 98]
```

The reduce method applies the function pairwise to all elements, returning a single value. The next example finds the sum of the numbers in an array.

```
a = [1, 2, 3, 4, 5];
asum = a.reduce((x, y) => x + y);
// asum = 15
```

3.11.8 Prototypes

Every object has a ***prototype***, which is another object that "stands behind it," or that it is "based on." If not otherwise specified, an object's prototype is Object.

Here is our running example:

```
let myCar = {make: "Subaru", year: 2018};
```

If we call myCar.toString(), we get the string "[object Object]". While this isn't very useful, it does show that myCar has a toString method. Where did it come from? It came from Object, which is a prototype for all objects.

If we use a for/in loop to print myCar we will see its make and year, but will not see the toString property of its prototype. The for/in loop only loops through the direct properties of an object, not the properties inherited from its prototype.

We can get the prototype of an object:

```
let proto = Object.getPrototypeOf(myCar);
```

and having gotten it, we can add features to it.

```
proto.style = "sedan";

proto.toString = function() {
  return this.year + " " + this.make; };
```

When we ask for a property of an object, be it a field like make or a method like toString, JavaScript first looks at the object itself. If it is found, that is what is used. If it isn't a property of the object, JavaScript looks for it in the object's prototype. If still not found, JavaScript looks in the prototype's prototype, and so on all the way up to Object. Eventually the property will be found or undefined will be returned.

Setting a property of an object sets the property on *that* object; it does not look at its prototype. If we set myCar.wheels = 4, the Car object is unaffected. Getting a value from an object will look up to its prototype if necessary, but setting a value never does.

3.11.9 Descriptors

Objects have properties and values, but the properties themselves have **descriptors**. The descriptors (or boolean *flags*) of a property are:

- enumerable — true if the property will be listed when we ask for the keys of an object, or when we loop over the properties.

- writable — true if the value can be changed.

- configurable — true if the property can be deleted or the flags modified.

  - Once a configurable flag is set to false, it cannot be changed back to true.

Our running example is

```
let car = {
```

```
        make: "Subaru", year: 2018,
        toString() { return this.year + " " + this.make; }
    }
```

When we loop over the properties of the car object, printing its keys and values, all of the fields that we defined (make, year, toString) will be processed because all three are enumerable by default.

```
for (let e in car) {
    console.log(e + "=" + car[e]);
}
```

The above code prints:

```
make=Subaru
year=2018
toString=toString() {
            return this.year + " " + this.make;
        }
```

These two methods operate on the descriptors:

- Object.getOwnPropertyDescriptor(*obj*, *property*);

- Object.defineProperty(*obj*, *property*, {*flag*: *boolean*, ...});

If we display the result of

```
Object.getOwnPropertyDescriptor(car, "year");
```

we get

```
[object Object] {
    configurable: true,
    enumerable: true,
    value: 2018,
```

```
    writable: true
}
```

If we don't want the toString method to appear when we loop over the car object, we can write

```
Object.defineProperty(car, "toString",
                      {enumerable: false,
                       configurable: false});
```

Setting enumerable to false keeps toFunction from being visible as a key of car (it still exists and can be used). Setting configurable to false prevents enumerable from ever being changed back to true.

3.11.10 Classes and Inheritance
3.11.10.1 Classes
A *class* describes a category of objects. It is a blueprint, or recipe, for making objects of that type. Classes are a relatively new addition to JavaScript, and are always in strict mode. Classes are based on prototypes, and provide little if any advantage over just using prototypes.

Here is the template for a class:

```
class ClassName {
  fields;
  constructor(arguments) {
    code
  }
  set name(value) {
    this.someOtherName = value;
  }
  get name() {
    return this.someOtherName;
  }
```

```
  methodName(arguments) {
    code
  }
}
```

Reminder: In a method (a function belonging to an object), this refers to the containing object. The same holds for constructors, setters, and getters.

A class has a **constructor** and may have some number of *fields*, *getters*, *setters*, and *methods*. To describe these, we will continue with our "car" example.

```
class Car {
  fuel = "gasoline"; // note: no "let"
  constructor(make, year) {
    this.make = make;
    this.year = year;
  }
}

let myCar = new Car("Subaru", 2018);
```

The word new calls the constructor. Within the constructor, make and year refer to the arguments of the constructor, while this. make and this.year are new fields belonging to the object being constructed. The constructor can be used to create other Car objects with different values.

Technical note: An object created from a constructor gets a constructor property, and that property has a name property, so myCar.constructor.name is "Car".

With the above definitions, the fields fuel, make, and year of myCar can be addressed directly, with myCar.fuel, myCar.make, and myCar.year. Sometimes, to provide a bit more "protection," a class can contain setters and getters. These are methods with the special syntax

```
set name(value) {…}    and
get name() {…}
```

A *setter* typically sets the value of a field. Setters are often used to check the legality of a value before saving it. It may save the information in a form other than the form provided to it (for example, miles may be converted to kilometers).

A *getter* typically returns the value of an object's field. Alternatively, a getter may compute a value in some other way and return it, for example, converting kilometers back to miles.

To use these setters and getters, *no change in the code* is involved. If a field has a setter, any attempt to change the value of a field (for example, myCar.make = "VW") will invoke that setter. Any attempt to read the value of a field will invoke its getter.

When a setter is defined for a variable, *every* attempt to set the value of that variable calls its setter. This can be a problem. In particular, the following code would cause an "infinite" recursion, as the setter calls itself.

```
set make(value) {
  this.make = value; // bad!
}
```

The recursion can be avoided by saving the variable under some other name. Since underscores are legal in variable names, one convention is to make a new name by prepending an underscore. This is only a convention; there is nothing special about underscores.

```
set make(value) {
  this._make = value; // okay
}
```

The new variable _make must be used throughout the class definition, while the old variable make should be used outside the class definition.

Getters and setters should normally be defined in pairs. Variables with setters must be stored under some other name, while variables without setters are unaffected.

> **Caution:** While the use of a setter can protect against accidentally changing a value, it is no protection against malicious users. With the above setter for make, the information is actually stored in a variable _make, and this variable is directly accessible.

A *method* is a function belonging to an object; and a class is a kind of object. Inside a class, a method is written like a function, except that the word function is omitted.

Here is an implementation of a Car class:

```
class Car {
  fuel = "gasoline";

  constructor(make, year) {
    this._make = make;
    this._year = year;
  }

  set make(arg) { this._make = arg; }

  get make() { return this._make; }
```

```javascript
set year(arg) {
  if (arg < 1903 ||
      arg > new Date().getFullYear()) {
    alert("Bad year: " + arg);
  }
  else {
    this._year = arg;
  }
}

get year() { return this._year; }

age() { // method
  let now = new Date().getFullYear();
  return now - this._year;
}

toString() {
  return this._year + " " + this._make;
}
}
```

An assignment to myCar will create an object with the fields make and year. After this, the test myCar instanceof Car will return true.

Caution: The word this is evaluated at run time, and depends on the context in which it occurs. Calling myCar. age() directly works fine, but myCar.age is an incomplete function with no fixed value for this. The solution is to replace the definition age() {...} with age = () => {...}, which creates a new age function for each Car.

3.11.10.2 Inheritance

Every class except Object *extends* (adds information to) some other class—its *superclass*. If no superclass is specified, as in Person, it defaults to extending Object.

A class may have any number of **subclasses**. A subclass builds upon ("extends") its superclass by adding or replacing features.

Here is a first example:

```
class Person {}  // extends Object

class Customer extends Person {}
```

When you ask JavaScript to create a new Customer, it starts by creating a new Object; then it then it adds to that object all the features of Person; finally, it adds all the features of Customer. In this way, an object of a class is built "on top of" an object of its superclass.

Every class must have a constructor, and the constructor should begin by calling the constructor for its superclass, with super(*args*). This isn't necessarily the very first thing that must be done, but it must happen before any use of this is attempted.

If no constructor is specified, JavaScript automatically supplies one. JavaScript assumes that the constructor will take the same arguments as the constructor in its superclass. If we could see it, it would look something like this:

```
constructor(...args) { super(...args); }
```

The **spread operator** (...) is used in the above both to collect an arbitrary number of arguments into an array and to supply an arbitrary number from an array.

Since the above classes have constructors, we can create objects with new Person() and new Customer().

Note: Although the classes Person and Customer have no properties or methods, they are not necessarily useless. Features can be added to them later, by assigning to the class *prototype*, for example, `Person.prototype.name = "anonymous";`.

An object created from a class is still just an object. You can, for example, add properties to it.

```
let friend = new Person();
friend.name = "Sally";
```

Technical note: The `instanceof` test will test for membership not only in the immediate class but also in all super-classes, so both `friend instanceof Person` and `friend instanceof Object` will return `true`.

With this in mind, let us revise the above classes so that every `Person` has a name and every `Customer` has an id. We will also provide a setter and a getter for a person's name, but insist that a name be a string.

```
class Person {
  constructor(name) {
    this._name = name;
  }

  set name(value) {
    if (typeof value == "string") {
      this._name = value;
    } else {
      alert(value + " is not a string.");
    }
  }

  get name() { return this._name; }
}

class Customer extends Person {
  constructor(name, id) {
    super(name);
```

```
    this.id = id;
  }
}
```

We can use these classes like this:

```
let person = new Person("Sally");
let cust = new Customer("Bill", 123);
cust.name = "William";
```

Note: Objects don't have to be created from a class in order to have getter and setter methods. The syntax, using the get and set keywords, is the same as that shown above.

3.11.10.3 Overriding Methods and Fields

Fields and methods defined in one class may be redefined, or ***overridden***, in a subclass. For example, the Object class defines a toString method. This method isn't very useful because it always returns "[object Object]", but it does exist.

You can override a method simply by defining a new method with the same name. For example, we might add the following method to the Person class:

```
toString() {
  return "My name is " + this.name";
}
```

Note: In most browsers, the console.log(*obj*) method *does not use* toString; instead, it prints the *structure* of the object. If this isn't what you want, you can call toString explicitly, or simply concatenate an empty string to the argument, console.log(*obj* + "").

Fields can also be overridden. However, the word this always refers to "the object before the dot." For example:

```
class Over {
  value = 100;
```

```
    show() {
      return "value is " + this.value;
    }
  }

  class Under extends Over {
    value = 50;
  }

  let under = new Under();
  console.log(under.show());
```

This prints "value is 50". Although show() is defined in Over, the variable under is of type Under, so this.value is 50, not 100.

If value were *not* defined in Under, then under would inherit it from Over, and this.value would be 100.

3.11.10.4 Class Prototypes

As noted earlier, you can construct an object that uses an existing object as its *prototype*.

```
let newObj = Object.create(oldObj);
```

The *newObj* will not initially have any properties of its own, but properties can be added later. Any attempt to look up a property of *newObj* will look first in *newObj* itself, but if not found there, JavaScript will look in its prototype, *oldObj*.

The method Object.getPrototypeOf(*newObj*) will return *oldObj*, but there is also an older way to access the prototype: *newObj*. __proto__ . The non-enumerable __proto__ property should not be used in new code.

Something similar happens with classes.

```
    class Person {…}
    class Customer extends Person {…}
    let sally = new Customer(…);
```

The object sally has access to the methods declared in Customer plus the methods declared in Person (unless they are overridden by methods with the same name in Customer).

When you declare a function or create a class with a constructor, that function or class gets a property confusingly named prototype. The value of this property is an object containing function names and definitions.

> **Note**: Do not confuse the prototype property of a class, *class*. prototype, with an object's prototype, *obj*. __proto__.

You can attach a method to all instances of a class by assigning to its prototype:

```
Person.prototype.initial = function() {
    return this.name[0];
}
```

The method initial will return the first character of a person's name (assuming that Person has a name property).

3.12 TRANSPILERS AND POLYFILLS

JavaScript evolves and (hopefully) gets better. Unfortunately, older browsers may not support some of the newest features. In order for JavaScript code to work "everywhere," there are two different approaches that may be taken:

1. Use only well-established features that work everywhere.

2. Use transpilers and/or polyfills.

A *transpiler* "compiles" newer syntactic features, such as the ?? operator, into older but equivalent syntax. **Babel** is a well-known transpiler.

A *polyfill* is a function or a library of functions that may or may not be currently included. A missing function can be added directly to the code. A library of polyfills may be loaded from a polyfill server, although this increases load time. There is more controversy about which polyfill library to use, if any, but **polyfill. io** is reasonably popular.

3.13 JSON

JSON (JavaScript Object Notation) is a way of representing data as text. This is useful for storing the data on a file, or transmitting it to or from a server. JSON is human-readable and editable; it is quite similar to data in JavaScript.

There are two methods:

- JSON.stringify(*value*)—Converts a JavaScript *value* to a JSON string.

- JSON.parse(*string*)—Converts a JSON *string* to a JavaScript object.

Both JSON methods can be given additional parameters, not described here, to modify values as they are processed.

Limitations:

- Functions, symbols, undefined, Infinity, and NaN cannot be represented in JSON. They are replaced by null.

- Dates are converted to strings, and not automatically converted back into Dates.

- Non-enumerable properties, and properties whose key is a symbol, are ignored.

Any object can be given a toJSON() method if the default representation is not satisfactory.

CHAPTER 4

Client-Side JavaScript

After a few introductory sections, the remainder of the book is divided into two parts: **Graphical User Interfaces**, which is all that many JavaScript programmers need, and **Using the DOM**, which describes the powerful understructure of web pages.

4.1 ESSENTIAL HTML

An **HTML page** is a text file, usually in Unicode, containing tags.

Most **tags** are containers. They consist of a **start tag**, some **contents**, and an **end tag**. The contents are the innerHTML of the tag. The syntax is:

<tagName> contents </tagName>

Container tags can contain text and other tags, to any level.

A few kinds of tags are *empty*, that is, not containers. For example, <br> is a line break, and <hr> is a horizontal rule. No end tag is needed. Such tags are sometimes written as *<tagName/>*.

An HTML page consists of at least four tags:

- A **document tag**, which identifies the file as HTML. It is not a container.

DOI: 10.1201/9781003359609-4

- An *html tag*, containing the head and body tags.

- A *head tag*, containing meta-information about the page, most of which is not displayed. This usually includes a <title> tag to name the page.

- A *body tag*, containing information to be displayed to the user, and numerous other tags to specify just how it should be displayed.

Here is a minimal HTML page.

```
<!DOCTYPE html>
<html>
  <head>
    <title>Example HTML Page</title>
  </head>
  <body>
    <p id="p1">The user sees this part.</p>
  </body>
</html>
```

Start tags can contain *attributes*, which have the form *name*="*value*". One such attribute is id, to assign a unique identifier to an individual tag.

JavaScript is case-sensitive, but tag names and attributes in HTML are not case sensitive.

Originally, all styling was done in the HTML itself. Today, most styles are applied by one or more associated *stylesheets*, written in CSS, Cascading Style Sheets.

4.2 ADDING JAVASCRIPT TO HTML

JavaScript can be added to an HTML page by:

- Putting the JavaScript within <script>...</script> tags, in either the head or the body.

- Putting the JavaScript in a separate file that has a .js extension, and loading it with <script src="*URL*.js"></script> in the head element. In this case, any code within the <script> tags will be ignored.

- Writing the JavaScript as the value of an HTML "event handler" attribute.

Function definitions are best placed in the <head> of the HTML document. Scripts in the <body> section are executed in order as the page is loaded, and typically produce output that is displayed at that point in the page.

Not everyone allows JavaScript to run in their browser. Text within a <noscript>*text*</noscript> tag will be displayed if and only if JavaScript is unavailable or disabled.

Large amounts of JavaScript and scripts that are used on more than a single page should be put in a file or files, not on the HTML page.

4.3 DOM OVERVIEW

The **HTML DOM** (**Document Object Model**) represents everything on the HTML page as a tree of Nodes, even the HTML comments and every bit of whitespace. Everything in the DOM is accessible to JavaScript and can be changed, and every change made by JavaScript is reflected immediately in the page as shown to the user. This is far more power than is needed for most applications.

Figure 4.1 shows the main subclasses of Node, not the structure of the DOM tree. The root of the DOM tree is a Node named document, of type Document, and it has one child, an Element representing the <html> tag. The document node has properties head and tail, which give access to the entire tree of nodes.

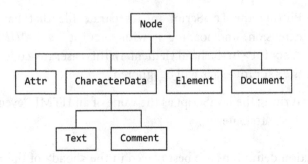

FIGURE 4.1 The DOM tree.

Every HTML tag is represented by an Element. An Element has a tagName, which is the name of the HTML tag. The name in the DOM is always uppercase: HTML, HEAD, BODY, TITLE, SCRIPT, and so on. Elements may have Attributes (another subclass of Node).

> **Note**: An Element is just one kind of Node, but it is so pervasive that the two are sometimes confused. Adding to the confusion, Element is a subclass of Node, so all the Node properties and methods can be used with Elements.

Because the nodes are in a tree structure, there are Node properties that allow movement in the tree: parentNode, firstChild, nextSibling, previousSibling, and lastChild.

Text and comments are represented by Text and Comment nodes, not Element nodes, so they do not show up in properties and methods that return only Elements. For example, an Element has a childNodes property that is a collection of all its children, and a children property that is a collection of only those children that are Elements.

In addition to the web page as described by the HTML, there are a large number of *events* happening all the time. Every keystroke, every mouse movement, and many other things cause events to occur. An interactive web page "listens for" and responds to a small subset of these events.

4.4 GRAPHICAL USER INTERFACES

A *Graphical User Interface*, or *GUI*, is a means of allowing the program to interact with a user. It typically consists of familiar controls, or *widgets*, such as buttons, text boxes, checkboxes, menu items, and the like.

GUIs can be used to create stand-alone programs, or they can be used to collect information to send back to a server (such as when ordering merchandise). A *form* is a container for widgets whose purpose is to collect information into a single bundle.

4.4.1 Events

GUI programs are different from other programs. Instead of one continuous sequence of code that runs from beginning to end, GUI programs are *event-driven*. When an "interesting" event occurs, some code is triggered to *handle* it. The code finishes, then nothing more happens until another "interesting" event occurs.

An "interesting" event is simply one that the programmer has written some code to handle. Events are happening all the time; practically anything that happens generates one or more events. The mouse moves over an HTML element? That's an event. The mouse moves out of an HTML element? That's another event. In fact, if the mouse moves at all, that's an event. There are over 70 kinds of events, all with names beginning with "on," such as onclick.

The key point is that events are happening all the time; the programmer doesn't have to do anything to create them. If the user clicks a button, that's an event that (normally) should be handled. If the user clicks a word in a paragraph, probably that event should be ignored. The programmer gets to decide which events to handle.

4.4.2 Widgets

Widgets are GUI elements. Each is represented by a tag in HTML, and a corresponding Element in the DOM. Typical widgets are buttons, text fields, text areas, checkboxes, radio buttons, scroll bars, and a number of other types.

Most GUI elements can be written using an <input> tag with a type attribute. If type is omitted, text is assumed; this is a box allowing one line of text to be entered.

Here are the possible values for type: button, checkbox, color, date, datetime-local, email, file, hidden, image, month, number, password, radio, range, reset, search, submit, tel (telephone), text, time, url, week.

There are a few widgets that have their own tag, rather than being a value of type: button, fieldset, label, option, optgroup, output, select.

4.4.3 Buttons

Buttons are *active elements*: When the user clicks a button, it should cause something to happen. Moreover, it is only polite to provide a visual cue that something has been done. For example, if the user clicks a Save button to save a file, and nothing visible occurs, the user may well get frustrated and click the button over and over again.

There are two ways to create a button:

```
<input type="button" value="Click me"
  onclick="alert('Hello')">

<button onclick="alert('Hello')">Click me
</button>
```

Each of these will appear on the web page as a button containing the words Click me. Each of them, when clicked, calls the alert function with the argument 'Hello'. The <button> tag requires a closing tag; the <input> tag does not. The <button> tag is newer and more flexible; for example, its innerHTML can be an image (using the <img> tag, rather than just text.

```
<button onclick="alert('Ouch!')">
   <img src="band-aid.png"></button>
```

The value of the onclick property should be a string containing JavaScript code, to be executed when the button is clicked—this is an *event handler*. Typically an event handler is a single function call, so that all substantive JavaScript code can be kept in one place rather than scattered throughout the HTML page. In the above examples, the function called is the alert function.

Note: The JavaScript code in an event handler must be a quoted string. Since the code itself may contain quoted strings, two kinds of quotes are commonly used, such as single quotes within double quotes.

The text on a button can be changed by JavaScript. For buttons defined with an input tag, the button's text is in its value attribute; for buttons defined with the button tag, the button's text is in its innerHTML.

4.4.4 Finding Widgets

There are a number of ways to specify a particular widget. Here are two:

- document.getElementById("*id*") — Returns the one element on the page whose tag has the attribute id="*id*". Ids must be unique on the page.

- document.getElementsByTagName("*tagName*") — Get an indexable collection of all the elements on the page with the given *tagName*.

There are two commonly used types of *collection* in the DOM. The `getElementsByTagName` method returns a *live* `HTMLCollection` of elements, while the `childNodes` property of a node is a *live* `NodeList` of nodes.

Both types of collection have a `length` property, and both can be indexed like an array or (redundantly) by the `item(`*index*`)` method. The fact that these are *"live"* means that they can be thought of as a window into the DOM, rather than a snapshot. If the DOM tree is changed, for instance by insertion or deletion of nodes, the contents and length of these collections change correspondingly. All `HTMLCollections` are live, but some `NodeLists` are *static*—they don't change as the DOM tree changes.

The method `Array.from(`*collection*`)` returns a static array of values from the *collection*.

4.4.5 Text Fields

A text field is a *passive element*. Clicking on it or entering text into it should not cause anything to happen. Later actions, such as button clicks, can access and use the text that was entered.

> **Note**: Technically, any element can be made active. You *can* put an `onclick` property in a text field, and it will work; but there is almost no situation in which this would be a good idea.

For text fields, there isn't a `<text>` tag, just a variation on the `<input>` tag.

```
<input type="text" size="12" value="Initial text">
```

The `size` attribute is a measure of how many characters can be displayed in the text field; it defaults to 20. Any number of characters can be entered into a text field, regardless of how many are displayed at a time.

Here's how to read what the user has entered. First, find the text field (perhaps by using document.getElementById), then read its value entry.

```
<input id='tx1' type="text">
<br>
<input type="button"
        value="Look in text field"
        onclick="alert('You entered: ' +
          document.getElementById('tx1').value)">
```

This works as you might expect. Enter something in the text field, click the button, and it shows up in an alert message.

In general, widgets should do nothing more complicated than call a single function. The above code can be written more cleanly by putting the function in the head of the document:

```
<script>
  function showText(id) {
    var field = document.getElementById(id);
    alert('You entered: ' + field.value);
  }
</script>
```

The handler for the button can then be written as a simple function call.

```
<input type="button" value="Look in text field"
        onclick="showText('tx1')">
```

4.4.6 Buttons and Forms

A common use for JavaScript is to send information to a server. Usually there is more than one piece of information: name, address, credit card number, and so on. To collect multiple pieces of information into a single submission, a form is used.

A *form* is a container, with start tag <form> and end tag </form>. The purpose is to contain various widgets, such as buttons and text fields, but any valid HTML can also be included. By default, enclosing HTML in a <form> does not make any visible difference on the screen.

We have already described the standard button type, using either <button> or <input type="button">. There are two other button types particularly relevant to forms. Each has an old version (with <input>) and a newer form (with <button>). For comparison, we show all three kinds of buttons here. First, the old way:

```
<input type="button" value="Click me">
<input type="submit" value="Send it">
<input type="reset" value="Forget it">
```

Then, the new way:

```
<button type="button">Click me</button>
<button type="submit">Send it</button>
<button type="reset">Forget it</button>
```

The old way puts the text of the button in a value property, so it can only be text. The new way puts it between <button> and </button>, so it can be almost anything.

- When a "plain" button (type="button") is clicked, no default action occurs.

- A *submit button* has the default text Submit, and the default action of sending all the information on the enclosing form to the server. (More on this shortly.)

- A *reset button* has the default text Reset, and the default action of clearing everything on the form to its original values. This action tends to annoy users.

Note: A button without an explicit type attribute behaves like type="button" *except in a form*, where it behaves like a type="submit" button.

One very convenient feature of forms is that they define a scope. Any widget within a form can have a name property, and this name can be used by other widgets in the same form. For example:

```
<form>
    <input name='tx1' type="text">
    <input type="button"
        value="Look in text field"
        onclick="alert('You entered: ' + tx1.value)">
</form>
```

An id must be unique on the entire HTML page and can be accessed by calling getElementById(*id*) from within scripts; a name should be unique within a form, and can be accessed directly by other widgets in the same form. Any widget can have a name and an id.

There is seldom any need for more than one form on a page, so it can be referenced by document.getElementsByTag Name("form")[0], or by its id if it has one. It is possible to have more than one form on a page, but forms may not be nested; that is, you cannot have a form inside a form.

A submit button within a form will, when clicked, submit that form. Outside a form, a submit button can use the attribute form="*formId*" to submit the form with that id.

Caution: If a form has a submit button, pressing Enter when in an input field of the form will also submit the form.

4.4.7 Form Verification

When a user clicks a Submit button, it usually makes sense to check the information in the form before sending it to the server. Not everything can be checked, of course, but many things can. Have any required fields been left blank? Are there unexpected characters in numeric fields? Does a credit card number have the right number of digits?

If a tag `<input type="text" ...>` contains the attribute `required` (with no value, just the word `required`), attempting to submit that form will cause the text field to be checked to make sure it is not blank. If it is blank, a small pop-up will appear next to the text field containing the words "Please fill in this field."

A text field may have an attribute `pattern="`*regexp*`"` to specify by a regular expression *regexp* exactly what may be entered into the text field; it will be checked when the Submit button is clicked. An erroneous entry will be flagged with "Please match the requested format." The *regexp* is given as a string, not bounded by slashes.

A text field may have a `placeholder="`*text*`"` attribute; the *text* is displayed as a hint to the user about what should be entered. The *text* will disappear when the user types into the field but reappears if the field becomes blank again.

One way to do arbitrary validation testing is to put an `onsubmit` property in the `<form>` tag, with a value that has the syntax `return` *function_call*; for example,

```
<form onsubmit="return validate()">
  Type a number:
  <input name='num' type="text">
  <br>
  <input type="submit">
</form>
```

In this example, the function validate() will be called when the submit button is clicked. If validation fails, the function should call event.preventDefault(), otherwise the submission will succeed. Either way, it is appropriate to inform the user.

4.4.8 Form Submission

When a form is submitted, the action attribute of the form tag tells the program *where* to send the data, and the method attribute tells *how* to send the data.

A form tag may contain action="*URL*" (Uniform Resource Locator) specifying the URL to which the information is to be sent. If the action property is not present, the URL of the page containing the form is used.

The two most commonly used values of the method attribute are "get" and "post".

4.4.8.1 Get Requests

A **get request**, <form method="get">, is a simple request for information. It should not be used when sending the data might change something on the server. For example, it should never be used to place orders.

The form data is appended to the URL with the syntax **?*name=value&name=value&...***, for example, google.com/search? q=octopus. Because the information is visible in the URL and can remain in the browser history, a get request should never be used for sensitive information.

If the method attribute is omitted, it defaults to get.

URLs are limited to 2048 ASCII (*not* Unicode) characters, so this limits the amount of data that can be submitted. For larger amounts of information, post must be used.

Get requests can be bookmarked.

4.4.8.2 Post Requests

A ***post request***, `<form method="post">`, is typically used for everything except simple requests for information. Data is sent in the body of the request, not in the URL, so large amounts of data can be sent. In the body, it has the form ***name=value&name=value&...*** . File uploads have a more complex structure.

A post request is more secure than a get request because it is not visible in the URL, not cached, and does not remain in the browser's history.

4.4.8.3 Other Requests

There are a few other method request types, such as head to request just the head of a page but not the body, and put to ask the server to store data.

It is up to the server which method requests it will accept and process. For example, a server might accept get requests but not post requests.

Code on the server side may be written in almost any language. Server-side coding is beyond the scope of this book.

4.4.9 Additional Text Widgets

A number of other widgets besides `<input type="text">` allow text input. All of the following except textarea are written as `<input type="type">`.

- password — All characters in the password field are displayed as bullets. This difference affects only what the user sees; entered text is recorded and can be accessed as usual.

- search — This is like `<input type="text">` but has a small icon in the right end that can be clicked to select previous entries in the field.

- email — A text field in which an email address can be entered. The entry is automatically checked (when submitted) to ensure that it contains the @ character. If the widget contains the multiple flag, more than one email address can be entered, separated by commas.

- number — A text field in which an integer can be entered. It is provided with up and down arrows for adding or subtracting one from the displayed number. If the value attribute is provided, it is used as the initial number displayed.

- **URL** — A text field in which a URL can be entered. The field is automatically checked (when submitted) to ensure that the entry is a syntactically correct URL.

- textarea — The <textarea name="*name*" rows="*nrows*" cols="*ncols*"> widget provides a multiline text-entry area, consisting of *nrows* rows and wide enough to display *ncols* characters.

  - A closing tag </textarea> is required. Text between the opening and closing tags (the innerHTML) is what is initially displayed in the text area.

  - Text in the text area will be displayed in a monospace font.

  - If the name attribute is omitted, the data in the text area will not be included when the form is submitted.

Some additional input widgets are available for choosing dates and times, but these are not yet supported on all browsers.

- date — For choosing a calendar date.

- time — For choosing a time of day.

- datetime-local — For choosing a date and time.

- week — For choosing a week.

4.4.10 Other Input Widgets

Along with button, text, submit, and password, there are a number of other values that the type attribute of an <input> tag can take. Recall that for <input>, all the needed information is in the start tag; no end </input> tag is used.

Many of these widgets give no indication to the user what they are intended for, so they should always be accompanied by a label, preferably with one that includes the for attribute.

- radio — The widget <input type="radio" id="*id*" name="*group*" value="*value*"> defines a radio button. Radio buttons are always used in groups, where every radio button has the same value for the name attribute. Selecting one radio button of a group deselects all the others in that group.

  - In a form, *group*.value is the value of the selected radio button. If not in a form, the radio buttons must be checked individually.

  - If no radio button has been selected, the value of that group is the empty string. To start with one button checked, give it the checked flag.

- checkbox — The <input type="checkbox" id="*id*"> widget is displayed as a small square that can be checked or unchecked, independently of any other checkboxes. The checked attribute (not the value attribute) of a checkbox will be true or false.

- file — The <input type="file"> widget displays a rectangle containing the words "Choose File". When clicked, it brings up a file chooser. The file chosen is accessible as the value attribute of the field. If the widget contains the multiple flag, multiple files can be selected.

- image — The <input type="image" src="*path*"> widget displays the indicated image.

- color — The <input type="color"> widget displays a small rectangle containing a color (black, by default). Clicking it brings up a color chooser. The value attribute sets the initial color, which must be of the form "#*RRGGBB*" (six hex digits representing the amounts of red, green, and blue).

- <input type="hidden"> widget is not visible to, and cannot be modified by, the user.

    - When interaction with a server occurs in a sequence of pages, the server can collect information from one page and store it as attributes of a hidden widget in the next page. In this way, a server can maintain information for a given user across a series of transactions.

    - Hidden fields are not a security device. The underlying HTML of a page, including hidden fields, can be viewed in any browser.

- <input type="range"> displays a slider, to be used for choosing a number in a given range. The default attributes are min="0", max="100", step="1", and value="50".

Usually each checkbox and radio button has an associated label immediately to its right. Checkboxes and radio buttons are small and a bit difficult to click on, so each should have a label with a for="*id*" attribute.

- <label for="*id*">*text*</label> — Clicking on the label is the same as clicking on the widget whose id is specified by the for attribute.

4.4.11 Events

User actions (typing something, moving the mouse, clicking the mouse, etc.) cause **events** to occur. One or more **event handlers** will be executed when certain events occur.

Each form element ("widget") can have attributes that act as event handlers. For example, a button may be defined as follows:

```
<input type="button" onclick="save()" value="Save">
```

Here, onclick is an event handler that tells JavaScript what to do; in this case, call the save() function when the button is clicked. Event handlers should generally be implemented as function calls.

Numerous events can occur, and not every widget can respond to every event. Browsers differ somewhat in which form elements will handle which events. This section describes the events and which form elements should be able to handle them.

Event names are sometimes written in camelCase, for example onClick instead of onclick. This works because tags are in HTML, which is case insensitive, but does not work in the quoted JavaScript, which is case sensitive.

The following events can be handled in <body> or <frame> elements (a *frame* is a separate URL file that is loaded as a part of a page):

- onload — the document or frame has completed loading. This can be used to execute a function to do any initialization required.

- onunload — the document or frame is unloaded. This can be used to perform any final cleanup actions.

The following events can be handled by most elements.

- onclick — the element is clicked. Buttons will almost always handle an onclick event. Most other widgets handle all the usual actions automatically for the given type of widget.

- ondblclick — the element is clicked twice in close succession.

- onmousedown — one of the mouse buttons (or the keyboard equivalent) is pressed while over the widget. To distinguish which mouse button is pressed, use onmousedown instead of onclick. The value of event.button will be 0, 1, or 2 for the left, middle, and right mouse buttons, respectively.

- onmouseup — the mouse button is released while over the widget. This event is usually ignored in favor of handling the onclick event

- onmouseover — the mouse is moved over the widget.

- onmouseout — the mouse is moved away from the widget.

- onmousemove — the mouse is moved.

Modern devices may have touch screens or pens. The above onmouse events may be replaced with onpointer events which work equally well with both mouse and touch events.

The following events can be handled by the body element and the input and textarea widgets.

- onkeypress — a key is clicked while this widget has focus.

- onkeydown — a key is depressed while this widget has focus.

- onkeyup — a key is released while this widget has focus.

- onfocus — the widget gains focus (for example, by the user tabbing to it).

- onblur — the widget loses the focus.

- onchange — the widget loses focus with a different value than it had when it gained focus.

The following events are often handled in the enclosing `<form>` tag.

- onselect — a portion of text is selected. To retrieve the selected text, use document.getSelection().

- onreset — the user has clicked a Reset button. If the value of the onreset attribute is "return false" or "return *someFunction*()" where *someFunction* returns false, the reset is cancelled.

- onsubmit — the user has clicked a Submit button. If the value of the onsubmit attribute is "return false" or "return *someFunction*()" where *someFunction* returns false, the submission is cancelled.

The following events are usually handled by the `<img>` tag.

- onabort — image loading has been interrupted.

- onerror — there was an error loading the image.

Event handlers have access to an event variable. In the handler:

- event.type is the part after "on" (e.g. for onclick, event.type is "click").

- event.target is the widget at which the event occurred.

- event.currentTarget is the current widget, when, as a result of bubbling (see next section), the immediate target does not handle the event.

- For mouse clicks, event.clientX and event.clientY indicate the mouse position; event.button is 0, 1, or 2 for left click, middle click, and right click, respectively.

- For key presses, event.key holds the character typed.

For example, the following code displays a button which, when clicked, writes a message to console.log:

```
<input type="button" value="Wow!" id="bait"
 onclick="console.log(event.type +
                    event.target.id);">
```

4.4.12 Bubbling

When an event happens on an element, the element can either handle it or ignore it. Either way, the element's *parent element* then gets a chance to handle the event, then the parent's parent, and so on, all the way up to the root (the global object). This process is called **bubbling**, and is generally desirable.

For example, if a button is clicked, and the button is in a form, and the form is in a document, and the document is in a window, any or all of these elements can do something in response to the button click.

- event.target is the most deeply nested element, and the one that first has a chance to respond.

- event.currentTarget is the one currently handling the event (it is equal to this).

- event.stopPropagation() stops any further bubbling. Not generally recommended.

- event.preventDefault() prevents default actions from occurring, such as form submission or following a link.

4.5 USING THE DOM

4.5.1 The Window Object

It is easy to think of document as the root of the HTML tree. In a browser, document is actually a child of another node, window. It is not necessary to say window.document, because window is assumed by default.

The window object is an indexable collection of *frames* or *iframes*; it is of zero length if these features are not used.

Windows, like documents, have properties and methods.

4.5.1.1 Window Properties

Here are some of the properties of a Window object. With the exception of location, all of these properties are read only.

- window — A self-reference to the current window (not usually needed). Programmer-defined global variables are actually properties of this object.

- self, frames, globalThis — On the web, these are all the same as window.

- length — The number of frames contained in this window.

- parent — If in a frame, the immediately enclosing window.

- document — The HTML document being displayed in this window.

- top — If in a frame, the outermost enclosing window.

- location — The URL of the document being displayed in this window. If you set this property to a new URL, that URL will be loaded into this window. Calling location.reload() will refresh the window.

- navigator — A reference to the browser object. Some properties of navigator are:

  - appName — the name of the browser, such as Netscape.

  - platform — the computer running the browser, such as Win32 or MacIntel.

  - userAgent — A detailed description of the platform.

4.5.1.2 Window Methods

Here are some of the available methods on windows.

- alert(***string***) — Displays an alert dialog box containing the string and an OK button.

- confirm(***string***) — Displays a confirmation box containing the string along with Cancel and OK buttons. Returns true if OK is pressed, false if Cancel is pressed.

- prompt(***string***) — Displays a prompt box containing the string, a text field, and Cancel and OK buttons. Returns the string entered by the user if OK is pressed, null if Cancel is pressed.

- ***window*** = open(***URL***) — Opens a new window containing the document specified by the URL.

- ***window***.close() — Closes the given window, but only if it was opened by open.

- ***timeoutId*** = setTimeout(***function, delay, arg1, ..., argN***) — Sets a timer to call the ***function*** with optional arguments ***arg1*** through ***argN*** after ***delay*** milliseconds. Returns a numeric ***timeoutId***.

- clearTimeout(***timeoutId***) — Cancels a pending timeout started by setTimeout.

- ***intervalId*** = setInterval(***code, interval***) — Sets a timer to execute the ***code*** (which may be a function or a string) every ***interval*** milliseconds. Returns a numeric ***intervalId***.

- clearTimeout(***intervalId***) — Cancels the periodic execution of code started by setInterval. This is the same method as the one above to clear a timeout id.

Note: To be technically correct, it should be noted that the timeout and interval methods available to windows are not defined in the Window object, but inherited from elsewhere. This makes little practical difference.

4.5.1.3 *Window Example*

Suppose we have the following JavaScript code (enclosed in <script> tags) in the head of the HTML document:

```
"use strict";
let win2, timer;

function display(str) {
  let e = document.getElementById("para");
  e.innerHTML = str;
}

function google(str) {
  console.log(window);
  win2 = window.location =
    "https://google.com" + "?q=" + str;
}

function googleIt() {
  display("Going to Google in 5 seconds.");
  let term =
    document.getElementById("search").value;
  timer = setTimeout(google, 5000, term);
}

function cancel() {
  display("");
  clearTimeout(timer);
}
```

and in the body:

```
<button onclick="googleIt()">Google</button>
<input type="text" id="search">
```

```
<button onclick="cancel()">Cancel</button>
<br>
<p id="para"></p>
```

When the HTML page is loaded, it shows a button labeled Google, a text field, and a second button labeled Cancel.

When the first button is clicked, it calls the googleIt() function. That function calls display to find the Element with the id "para," which is an initially empty paragraph, and sets it to contain the text "Going to Google in 5 seconds." Then the googleIt() function finds the text field with the id "search" and gets its text into a variable named term. Finally, googleIt sets a timer that will call the google function with the argument term after 5 seconds (5000 milliseconds).

Note: This will only work if the browser permits it, which depends on the browser's settings.

If the Cancel button is clicked within five seconds, the cancel method will erase the text in the paragraph whose id is "para", then cancel the timer (whose id has been saved in the global variable timer). Consequently, the timer event will not occur, and google() will not be called.

If the Cancel button is not clicked, the google function will try to open a browser tab to google.com, with the search term passed to it as an argument, and will save the window id in a global variable named win2.

Note: The ? appended to the URL provides information to the server as *name=value* pairs. Multiple *name=value* pairs are separated by ampersands (&). Google recognizes, among other names, q for "query."

4.5.2 The Document Object

A *document* represents an HTML page.

The name window refers to the window displaying the HTML; window.document refers to the HTML in that window (or more accurately, the tree of Nodes representing that HTML). Document properties and methods must be prefixed by document..

The constructor new Document() will return a new HTML page, complete with an empty head and body.

4.5.2.1 Document Properties

Here are a few of the properties of document:

- document.documentElement — An HTMLHtmlElement whose innerHTML is the text of the <html> tag.

- document.head — An HTMLHeadElement whose innerHTML is the text in the document's <head>.

- document.body — An HTMLBodyElement whose innerHTML is the text in the document's <body>.

- document.title — The document's title, as a string.

- document.URL — The document's read-only URL as a string, including the protocol (such as http://).

- document.bgColor — The background color of the document; may be changed by assignment. The assigned value should be a string such as "red", "#ff0000", or "ff0000", not a JavaScript-style hexadecimal number.

- document.fgColor — The foreground (text) color of the document, assignable in the same way as bgColor.

The purpose of HTML has always been to describe the *structure* of a document, but from the beginning it had a number of features to control style. Modern HTML has deprecated many of these, with style elements (colors, borders, fonts, etc.) being described instead by **CSS**, **Cascading Style Sheets**. There are a huge number of style attributes; below is a brief sampling.

```
document.body.style.backgroundColor = "#EEEEEE"
document.body.style.color = "#999999"
document.body.style.border = "thick solid #0000FF";
document.body.style.borderColor = "#00ff00";
document.body.style.fontFamily = "Courier New, Impact"
document.body.style.fontSize = "24pt"
```

In order, these (1) set the background color to light gray, (2) set the text color to a hard-to-read dark gray, (3) set the border around the entire document to a thick blue line, (4) change the border color to green, (5) set the font to Courier New if available, or Impact if Courier New is not available, and (6) set the font size to 24 points.

Note: In JavaScript, a hex number is written as 0x**digits** or 0X**digits**. In HTML, a hex number is written as the string #**digits**. Allowable digits are 0 to 9 and A to F (or a to f).

The above examples used document.body, but any selectable Element can be used. Again, the use of CSS is preferred.

4.5.2.2 Finding Nodes

To manipulate the DOM, it is necessary to be able to find specific elements. For example, a button click may need to find, read, and use the contents of a particular text field. There are several ways this can be done.

- document.getElementById(**id**) — Returns the Element with the property id="**id**". Ids must be unique within the page.

- document.getElementsByTagName(**tagName**) — Returns a live collection of all the Elements with the given **tagName**.

- `document.getElementsByClassName(`*className*`)` — Returns an HTMLCollection of all the Elements that have the property class="*className*".

Note: The `class` attribute of an HTML tag is used to apply a named CSS style to the HTML element.

- `document.querySelector(`*selector*`)` — Returns the first element within the document that is matched by the CSS *selector*. The *selector* is given as a string.

- `document.querySelectorAll(`*selector*`)` — Returns all elements within the document that are matched by the CSS *selector*. The *selector* is given as a string.

Some selectors are:

- *tagName* — To select all elements with the given *tagName*.

- *#id* — To select the one specific element with the given *id*.

- *.className* — To select all elements with the attribute class="*className*". Notice the initial period.

- *tagName.className* — To select all elements that have the given *tagName* and also have the attribute class="*className*".

- * — To select all elements.

- *selector1, selector2* — To select all elements of type *selector1* and all elements of type *selector2*.

- *selector1 > selector2* — To select all elements of type *selector2* that are children of elements selected by *selector1*.

- *selector1 selector2* — To select all elements of type *selector2* that are descendants (children, children of children, etc.) of elements selected by *selector1*.

- *selector1* ~ *tagName2* — To select all elements of type *selector2* that are subsequent (later) siblings of *selector1* elements.

- *selector1* + *selector2* — To select each element of type *selector2* that immediately follows (is the next sibling of) *selector1* elements.

Some properties are returned as an HTMLCollection (list) of the corresponding elements. Individual elements can be accessed with brackets or with the index function, for example, document. forms[0] or document.forms.item(0).

- document.embeds — A list of the <object> elements.

- document.forms — A list of all the <form> elements.

- document.images — A list of all the <img> elements.

- document.links — A list of all the hyperlinks (the <a> and <area> elements that have an href attribute).

- document.scripts — A list of all the <script> elements.

4.5.2.3 Creating Nodes
You have already met the document methods for finding nodes. Here are some methods for creating nodes.

- *document*.createElement(*tagName*) — Returns a new Element with the given *tagName*.

- *document*.createAttribute(*name*) — Returns a new attribute with the given *name*. A value can be assigned to it later.

- *document*.createComment(*text*) — Returns a new comment node with the given *text*.

- ***document*.**createTextNode(***text***) — Returns a new Text node with the given ***text***.

- ***node*.**cloneNode(***deep***) — Returns a copy of ***node***; if ***deep*** is true, all ancestors (the complete subtree of ***node***) is also copied.

Once nodes are created, they can be added to the document with Node methods.

4.5.3 Node Objects

As noted earlier, everything on an HTML page is represented in the DOM, and accessible from the variable named document, which is of type Document. The Document class is a subclass of the Node class. Other subclasses of Node are CharacterData, Element, and Attr.

The type hierarchy is large and complex. Fortunately, it is usually sufficient to think of the DOM as a tree of Nodes, most of which are Elements. Most useful is document.body, which is the root of the entire <body> subtree.

4.5.3.1 Node Properties

Here are some of the properties of a Node:

- parentNode, firstChild, nextSibling, previousSibling, and lastChild are read-only properties that allow movement from one Node to another.

- ownerDocument — The Document to which the Node belongs.

- nodeType is an integer denoting the type of node. There are 12 types; 1 for elements, 2 for attributes, 3 for text, 9 for documents, and several others.

- `children` — A live `HTMLCollection` of all the child nodes of this node which are `Elements`. Other node types are not included.

- `childNodes` — A live `NodeList` of all the child nodes of this node, regardless of type.

- `textContent` — The complete text of the `Node` and all its descendants, minus the HTML tags. In other words, the unstyled text as it would be seen on the screen.

Note: Replacing the `innerHTML` of an `Element` will cause the new text to be parsed as HTML, while replacing its `textContent` will result in the new text being displayed as written.

4.5.3.2 Node Methods

Nodes can be added, replaced, or deleted. Here are some of the methods of a Node:

- *node*.before(*sibs*) — Inserts *sibs* as siblings (children of the same node) just before *node*.

- *node*.prepend(*children*) — Inserts *children* as children of *node* before any existing children.

- *node*.append(*children*) — Inserts *children* as children of *node* after any existing children.

- *node*.after(*sibs*) — Inserts *sibs* as siblings (children of the same node) just after *node*.

- *node*.replaceWith(*replacements*) — Replaces *node* with some number of replacement nodes or strings.

- *node*.remove() — Removes *node*.

In the above, the arguments (*sibs*, *children*, *replacements*) may be one or more nodes or strings. Strings will be inserted as text nodes.

Removing or replacing a node also removes or replaces all the descendants of that node.

4.5.4 Elements

Every tag in an HTML page is represented by an `Element` object in the DOM tree, and every attribute in a tag is represented by an `Attribute` object in the DOM. Modifications to a DOM object are immediately reflected in the appearance of the HTML page.

4.5.4.1 Element Properties

Here are some of the properties of an `Element`:

- *element*.tagName — The read-only name of the tag, in uppercase (e.g. "HEAD").

- *element*.innerHTML — The text between the start tag and end tag.

- *element*.outerHTML — A string consisting of the start tag, the innerHTML, and the end tag.

- *element*.attributes — A NamedNodeMap (see below) of the attributes of *element*.

A NamedNodeMap is a live collection of `Attr` objects. (Despite the name, this is the only kind of `Node` in a `NamedNodeMap`.) It is array-like, but is *not* an array. It has a `length` property, and can be indexed into like an array.

4.5.4.2 Element Methods

Here are some of the methods of an `Element`:

- *element*.hasAttributes() — Returns true if *element* has attributes.

- *element*.getAttributeNames() — An array (possibly empty) of the names of the attributes of *element*.

- *element*.hasAttribute(*name*) — Returns true if *element* has the given attribute.

- *element*.getAttribute(*name*) — Returns the value of the named attribute as a string. If the named attribute does not exist, the value returned is either null or the empty string, depending on the browser.

- *element*.setAttribute(*name*, *value*) — Adds or updates the value of the named attribute.

- *element*.removeAttribute(*name*) — Removes an attribute from the *element*.

An Attr is a Node that represents the attributes of an HTML tag. It has name and value properties.

A document is a node, but not an element; this results in some duplication of code within the DOM. The following methods are identical to methods of document, but search within the element rather than within the entire document.

- *element*.getElementsByTagName(*tagName*)

- *element*.getElementsByClassName(*className*)

- *element*.querySelector(*selector*)

- *element*.querySelectorAll(*selector*)

There is no equivalent of getElementById, since ids must be unique within the document.

HTML text can be parsed and inserted into the DOM with the following method:

- *element*.insertAdjacentHTML(*where*, *html*) — Parses the *html* and inserts the result into the DOM at the location specified by the string *where*, which is one of:

- "beforebegin" — Before *element*.

- "afterbegin" — As the first child of *element*.

- "beforeend" — As the last child of *element*.

- "afterend" — After *element*.

4.5.5 CharacterData

There are three kinds of CharacterData: Text, Comment, and ProcessingInstruction (not covered here). These have all the properties and methods of Node, plus the following:

- data — The text content.

- length — The number of characters in the text.

- nodeName — The string "#text".

- appendData(*data*) — Adds *data* to the end of the text.

- insertData(*offset*, *data*) — Inserts *data* into the text at the given *offset*.

- deleteData(*offset*, *count*) — Removes *count* characters from the *text*, starting at the given *offset*.

- replaceData(*offset*, *count*, *data*) — Replaces *count* characters starting at *offset* with *data*.

- substringData(*offset*, *count*) — Returns *count* characters from the text, starting at *offset*.

- remove() — Removes the node from the DOM tree.

4.5.6 Example: ShowTree

The following HTML page will, when the button is clicked, write out the complete tree of Elements to the console, though with severely abbreviated text. The console must be open to see the results.

```
1  <!DOCTYPE html>
2  <html>
3  <head>
4    <title>showTree Example</title>
5
6    <script>
7    function abbreviate(str) {
8      let oneLine = str.replaceAll(/\s+/g,
          " ").trim();
9      if (oneLine.length <= 45) return oneLine;
10     return "'" + oneLine.substr(0, 30) +
11         " … " + oneLine.substr(-8, 10) + "'";
12   }
13
14   function onlyWhitespace (str) {
15     return /^\s+$/.test(str);
16   }
17
18   function showTree(e, indent="") {
19     let s = indent + e.nodeName + " ";
20     if (e instanceof CharacterData) {
21       if (onlyWhitespace(e.textContent)) {
22         s += "[whitespace] ";
23       } else {
24         s += abbreviate(e.textContent);
25       }
26     }
27     if (e.hasAttributes) {
28       let attrs = e.attributes;
29       for (let i = 0; i < attrs.length; i += 1) {
30         if (attrs[i].value != null) {
31           s += attrs[i].name  + ":" +
32               attrs[i].value + " ";
33         }
34       }
35     }
36     if (e.innerHTML) {
```

```
37          s += abbreviate(e.innerHTML);
38        }
39        console.log(s);
40        for (node of e.children) {
41          showTree(node, indent + "|  ");
42        }
43      }
44    </script>
45  </head>
46
47  <body>
48    <!-- Steve Jobs quote -->
49    <p><i>Everyone</i> should learn how to program
50    a computer because it teaches you how to
          think.</p>
51    <button onclick="showTree(document)"> Show
          Tree</button>
52  </body>
53  </html>
```

Line 51 defines a button which, when clicked, will call the showTree method with the document node.

At line 19, showTree begins the creation of a string s, starting with some indentation and the tagName of the parameter.

Line 20 tests if the argument is CharacterData (either Text or Comment). If it is, either an abbreviated version of the text is added to s, or an indication that the text consists entirely of whitespace. As written above, with e.children in line 40, this code will never be used (but see below).

Lines 27 through 35 check if the argument has attributes, and if so, adds them to string s.

Lines 36 through 38 add an abbreviated version of the node's innerHTML, if it has one, and line 39 displays the result on the console.

The abbreviation of the innerHTML is done by lines 7 through 12. This abbreviation prevents the output from being several times as long as the original HTML.

Lines 40 to 42 get the children of the argument node e, all of which are Elements, and recur with some added indentation.

Here is the result:

```
#document
|   HTML '<head> <title>showTree Example … </body>'
|   |   HEAD '<title>showTree Example</title … /script>'
|   |   |   TITLE showTree Example
|   |   |   SCRIPT 'function abbreviate(str) {
              let … "); } }'
|   |   BODY '<!-- Steve Jobs quote --> <p>< … /button>'
|   |   |   P '<i>Everyone</i> should learn h … o think.'
|   |   |   |   I Everyone
|   |   |   BUTTON onclick:showTree(document) Show Tree
```

The duplication in the above is because elements contain other elements. For example, showTree Example is in a TITLE tag, which is in a HEAD tag, which is in an HTML tag, so it shows up three times. Some but not all whitespace has also been removed.

If e.children in line 40 is replaced with e.childNodes, then *all* child nodes of e, not just those that are Elements, nodes will be printed. This includes Text and Comment nodes.

Afterword

JavaScript was pressed into service by Netscape in 1995, during the "browser wars." It was initially named LiveScript, but the name was changed after only three months, probably because Java was quickly gaining in popularity. There is no real relationship between the two languages; the resemblance is because both languages borrowed heavily from C.

Microsoft responded in 1996 with a knock-off version called JScript.

Netscape submitted JavaScript to ECMA International, a standards organization, for standardization. Microsoft participated for a few years, then dropped its support. Subsequently, Firefox and Chrome gained a large enough market share to get Microsoft to rejoin the party. To make a long story short, standardization finally succeeded in 2009 with ECMAScript 5, and later with ECMAScript 6 in 2015. Subsequent versions (through 11) have only relatively minor changes.

The Oracle Corporation currently owns the name "JavaScript," so the official name of the language is ECMAScript.

The history of the HTML DOM follows a similar trajectory. Standards are currently maintained by the Web Hypertext Application Technology Working Group, https://whatwg.org/;

this is the ultimate source for complete, detailed information. More approachable documentation for HTML, CSS, and JavaScript can be found at MDN Web Docs, https://developer.mozilla.org/en-US/.

This book has attempted to provide a reasonably simple, coherent subset of JavaScript and the HTML DOM. Even so, the book is half again as long as I, your author, anticipated, and a great deal has been omitted. My hope is that it will provide a suitable starting point for your future studies.

Appendix A: Array Methods

Although negative array indices are not allowed, array *methods* can use negative numbers as indices, with -1 denoting the last location, -2 the next to last, and so on.

- Array.from(*iter*) — Creates and returns an array of values from an iterable object *iter*.

- Array.isArray(*obj*) — Tests if *obj* is an array.

- *array*.concat(*arg1*, ..., *argN*) — Creates and returns a new array with all the elements of the old array and also the elements *arg1*, ..., *argN*.

- *array*.flat(*depth*) — Removes one level of nesting from arrays of arrays (... of arrays).

- *array*.includes(*value*) — Tests if *value* occurs in *array*.

- *array*.join(*sep*) — Converts all the elements of the array to strings and concatenates them, using *sep* as a separator. If *sep* is omitted, commas are used. Holes, undefineds, and nulls are converted to empty strings.

- *array*.pop() — Removes and returns the last value in the array and decrements the length of the array.

- *array*.push(*value1*, ..., *valueN*) — Adds the values to the end of the array and returns the new length of the array.

- *array*.shift() — Removes and returns the first value in the array. Remaining elements are all shifted down one place.

- *array*.slice(*start*, *end*) — Returns a new array consisting of elements *start* through *end* - 1 of the original array.

- *array*.sort() — Sorts the array in place, in *alphabetical* (lexicographic) order; numbers are sorted according to their string representations, so 200 < 5.

- *array*.splice(*start*) — Removes all elements from index location *start* to the end of the array and returns them in a new array.

- *array*.splice(*start*, *count*) — Removes *count* elements from the array, starting at index location *start*, and returns them in a new array.

- *array*.splice(*start*, *count*, *value1*, ..., *valueN*) — Removes *count* elements from the array, starting at index location *start*, and replaces them with new elements *value1*, ..., *valueN*. The removed elements are returned in a new array.

- *array*.toString() — Creates and returns a comma-separated list of the string representations of each element in the array. This method may not show brackets, so a higher-dimensional array will appear one-dimensional.

- *array*.unshift(*value1*, ..., *valueN*) — Adds *value1*, ..., *valueN* to the beginning of the array; the return value is the new length of the array.

The JavaScript methods Math.min and Math.max each take an arbitrary number of arguments; they do *not* take arrays. However, the spread operator (...) will turn an array into a sequence of values, so Math.min(...*array*) and Math.max(...*array*) work fine.

Appendix B: Higher-Order Methods

There are a number of built-in array methods that take a function as a parameter. Arrow functions are often used as arguments, though functions defined in other ways may be used. In the following, we use *f* for a function that takes one argument and *f2* for a function that takes two arguments.

- *array*.sort(*f2*) — Sorts the array in place and also returns the sorted array. If *f2*(*x*, *y*) returns a negative result, *x* is considered to be less than *y*; if zero, equal; if positive, *x* is greater than *y*..

  - For example, a.sort((x, y) => x - y)) sorts the array a in ascending numeric order.

- *array*.forEach(*f*) — Calls the function *f* for each element of *array*. To be useful, *f* should have side effects, since any values returned by *f* are ignored.

- *array*.find(*f*) — Finds and returns the first value in *array* for which *f* returns a truthy value (or undefined if none is found)

- *array*.findIndex(*f*) — Finds and returns the first index of a value in *array* for which *f* returns a truthy value (or -1 if none is found).

- *array*.map(*f*) — Applies *f* to each element of *array*, returning an array of the results. Holes, if any, are preserved.

- *array*.flatMap(*f*) — Applies *f* to each element of *array*. If the resulting array is multidimensional, one level of nesting is removed, promoting all values to the next higher level.

- *array*.filter(*f*) — Returns an array containing all and only those values of *array* for which *f* returns a truthy value.

- *array*.reduce(*f2*, *initial*) — Given a function *f2* of two parameters, applies *f2* to *initial* and the first element of *array*, then applies *f2* to that result and the second element, and so on, resulting in a single value.

  - If *array* is empty, *initial* is returned.

  - If *array* is known to be nonempty, *initial* may be omitted.

  - For example, *array*((x, y) => x + y) returns the sum of all the elements of *array*.

- *array*.reduceRight(*f2*) — Like reduce, but works right to left instead of left to right.

- *array*.some(*f*) — Returns true if array contains at least one element for which *f* returns a truthy value.

  - *array*.every(*f*) — Returns true if *f* returns a truthy value for every element of the array.

Appendix C: String Methods

Here are some of the more important methods on strings. Strings are *immutable* (cannot be modified), hence all string methods return a new string.

- *string*.charAt(*n*) — Returns the *nth* character of a string. Same as *string*[*n*].

- *string*.charCodeAt(*n*) — Returns the numeric Unicode value of the *nth* character of a string.

- *string0*.concat(*string1*, ..., *stringN*) — Returns the concatenation (joining) of all the given strings.

- *string*.fromCharCode(*c1*, ..., *cN*) — Creates a string from the given numeric Unicode values.

- *string*.includes(*substr*) — returns true if *substr* occurs as a substring of *string*, otherwise false.

- *string*.includes(*substr*, *start*) — returns true if *substr* occurs as a substring of *string* starting at or after *start*, otherwise false.

- *string*.indexOf(*substring*) — Returns the position of the first character of *substring* in *string*, or -1 if not found.

- *string*.indexOf(*substring*, *start*) — Returns the position of the first character of *substring* in *string* that begins at or after position *start*, or -1 if not found.

- *string*.lastIndexOf(*substring*) — Returns the position of the first character of the last occurrence of *substring* in *string*, or -1 if the substring cannot be found.

- *string*.lastIndexOf(*substring*, *start*) — Returns the position of the first character of the last occurrence of *substring* in *string* that occurs at or before position *start*, or -1 if the substring cannot be found.

- *string*.match(*regexp*) — Returns an array containing the results of the regular expression match, or null if no match is found. On a successful match:

  - If the flag g is set, the array contains the matched substrings.

  - If g is not set, array location 0 contains the matched text, and remaining locations contain text matched by any parenthesized subexpressions. The array index property gives the position of the first character of the match.

- *string*.padEnd(*length*, *string2*) — Adds characters from *string2* to the end of *string* as many times as needed to form a new string of length *length*. If omitted, *string2* defaults to blanks. If *string* is already of length *length* or greater, the result is just *string*.

- *string*.padStart(*length*, *string2*) — Adds characters from *string2* to the beginning of *string* as many times as needed to form a new string of length *length*. If omitted, *string2* defaults to blanks. If *string* is already of length *length* or greater, the result is just *string*.

- **_string_**.repeat(**_n_**) — Returns a string consisting of **_n_** copies of **_string_**.

- **_string_**.replace(**_target_**, **_replacement_**) — Returns a string in which the first occurrence of **_target_** has been replaced by **_replacement_**.

  - The **_target_** may be either a string or a regular expression. If the g flag of a regular expression is set, all occurrences of **_target_** are replaced.

  - The **_replacement_** may be the name of a one-parameter function (_not_ a method). The function is applied to the matched **_target_** to get the actual replacement value.

- **_string_**.replaceAll(**_target_**, **_replacement_**) — Like replace, except that all occurrences of target are replaced. If **_target_** is a regular expression, the g flag _must_ be used (!).

- **_string_**.search(**_target_**) — Returns the index of the first character of a string that matches the string or regular expression **_target_**, or -1 if no such string can be found.

- **_string_**.slice(**_start_**, **_end_**) — Returns a substring of **_string_** starting at position **_start_** and ending position **_end_**-1. If **_end_** is omitted, all characters at and after **_start_** are returned. The arguments **_start_** and **_end_** may be negative: -1 is the last character of **_string_**, -2 is the next to last, and so on.

- **_string_**.split(**_string2_**) — Breaks **_string_** up into substrings using **_string2_** as a separator, and returns an array of the results. If **_string2_** is the empty string, an array of characters is returned. A regular expression may be used in place of **_string2_**.

- **_string_**.substr(**_start_**, **_length_**) — Returns a substring of at most **_length_** characters, starting from position **_start_** of **_string_**. If there are fewer than **_length_** characters remaining, all remaining characters will be returned. The argument *start* may be negative: -1 is the last character of *string*, -2 is the next to last, and so on.

- *string*.substring(*start, end*) — Returns a substring of *string* starting at position *start* and ending position *end*-1. If *end* is omitted, all characters at and after *start* are returned. Negative indices are treated as zeroes.

- *string*.toLowerCase() — Returns a lowercase version of *string*.

- *string*.toUpperCase() — Returns an uppercase version of *string*.

- *string*.trim() — Returns a string with initial and final whitespace removed.

- *string*.trimEnd() or *string*.trimRight() — Returns a string with final whitespace removed.

- *string*.trimStart() or *string*.trimLeft() — Returns a string with initial whitespace removed.

Appendix D:
Regular Expressions

Although each language may add its own flourishes, basic regular expressions are quite standardized across languages. Inside a regular expression there may be the following:

- *Literals* are characters that stand for themselves. Examples include letters, digits, and whitespace characters. The regular expression/cat/will try to match an occurrence of the word "cat."

- *Metacharacters* are characters that have special meaning in a regular expression. The metacharacters are: \ | ( ) [{ ^ $ * + . ?

- *Escaped characters* are characters that are preceded by a backslash in order to use them as literals rather than as metacharacters or because they are difficult to represent otherwise. For example, the question mark has a special meaning in a regular expression so if you want it to mean just the literal character, you have to escape it.: \?

Table A.1 lists the metacharacters and their meanings.

Table A.1

Expression	Meaning	Examples	Explanation
a literal character	That same character	M	The capital letter M
XY	An *X* followed by a *Y*	cat	The three characters c a t, in that order
[*XYZ*]	Any one of the characters *X*, *Y*, or *Z*.	b[aeiou]g	One of the words bag, beg, big, bog, or bug
[*X-Y*]	Any one character between *X* and *Y*, inclusive	[0-9] [a-zA-Z]	Any decimal digit; Any letter
[^*X-Y*]	Any one character not between *X* and *Y*, inclusive	[^a-zA-Z]	Any non-letter
X*	Zero or more occurrences of *X*	\s*	Any amount of whitespace
X+	One or more occurrences of *X*	\s+	At least one whitespace character
X?	An optional *X*	dogs?	Either dog or dogs
X{*n*,*m*}	From *n* to *m* occurrences of *X*	his{2,4}	hiss or hisss or hissss
X{*n*,}	*n* or more occurrences of *X*	his{2,}	hiss or hisss or hissss, and so on
X{*n*}	Exactly *n* occurrences of *X*	his{2}	Hiss
X|*Y*	Either *X* or *Y*	The (boy|girl)	Either The boy or The girl
^*X*	*X* at the beginning of the string	^[A-Z]	An initial capital letter (the ^ itself matches the empty string)

(Continued)

Table A.1 *(Continued)*

Expression	Meaning	Examples	Explanation
X$	*X* at the end of the string	[\.\?!]$	Ends with a period, question mark or exclamation point (the $ itself matches the empty string)
\b	The empty string between a word character (\w) and a nonword character (\W)	\bC\b	The word C, as in the language
\B	An empty string that is not between a word character (\w) and a nonword character(\W)	un\B	The initial part of the words unhealthy, undulate, etc.
(?=*pat*)	Look ahead to make sure that the pattern *pat* will match next, but do not count it in the matched part	\w+(?=)	A word, provided it is followed by a space
(?!*pat*)	Look ahead to make sure that the pattern *pat* will not match next	\w+(?!-)	A word, provided it is not followed by a hyphen
(*X*)	Group the expression *X* into a single unit, and remember what it matches	(\/\/.*$)	A //-style comment (keep for later reference)
(?:*X*)	Group the expression *X* into a single unit, but do not remember what it matches	(?:\/\/.*$)	A //-style comment (discard it)

Do not include extra spaces in regular expressions! A space is a literal character and a space in a regular expression requires a space in the string being searched.

A *character class* represents any one of the set of characters. There are several predefined character classes:

- \w A word character; same as [a-zA-Z0-9_]

- \W A nonword character; same as [^a-zA-Z0-9_]

- \s A whitespace character

- \S A non-whitespace character

- \d A digit; same as [0-9]

- \D A nondigit; same as [^0-9]

- (A period, not escaped) Any character except a line terminator

Other character classes can be described by using brackets. For example, the character class [aeiouAEIOU] could be used to recognize vowels.

A regular expression may be followed immediately by a flag. Two important flags are g for "global," meaning "do it everywhere," and i for "case insensitive."

References

Crockford, Douglas. *JavaScript: The Good Parts*. O'Reilly Media; 1st edition (May 1, 2008).

Flanagan, David. *JavaScript: The Definitive Guide: Master the World's Most-Used Programming Language*. O'Reilly Media; 7th edition (June 23, 2020).

References

Index

Printed in the United States
by Baker & Taylor Publisher Services